ND THE
N CLOUD

Union Carbide's Bhopal Massacre

by
Larry Everest

Banner Press • Chicago

Banner Press, P.O. Box 6469, Chicago, IL 60680

Library of Congress Cataloging-in-Publication Data

Everest, Larry.
  Behind the poison cloud.

    Bibliography: p.
    1. Bhopal Union Carbide Plant Disaster, Bhopal, India,
1984. 2. Industrial toxicology – India – Bhopal.
3. Pesticides industry – India – Bhopal – Accidents.
4. Methyl isocyanate – Environmental aspects – India –
Bhopal. 5. Union Carbide Ltd. (India) 6. Union
Carbide Corporation. I. Title.
HD7269.C452I524 1986   363.1'79   85-26863
ISBN 0-916650-26-X
ISBN 0-916650-25-1 (pbk.)

Contents

Preface

In early February 1985, two months after the industrial disaster in Bhopal, India, in which thousands died and tens of thousands more were severely injured as a result of a massive gas leak from Union Carbide Corporation's pesticide plant there, I traveled to India.

I was there for six weeks, visiting New Delhi and Bombay, and spending considerable time in Bhopal itself. I talked to Union Carbide employees – from high-level management to workers at the Bhopal plant. I interviewed a broad spectrum of doctors involved in the care of the victims, and Indian government officials, including those charged with enforcing environmental and safety regulations. I also talked with scientists investigating the disaster, Indian journalists, environmental activists, and members of volunteer organizations who came to Bhopal to aid the victims.

Finally, I talked with many of the people who live in the shanty colonies in the shadow of Union Carbide's Bhopal plant – the people who experienced the horror of December 2–3, 1984 first hand and who were among its main victims. I collected much of the available written information on the disaster, including Indian government reports, Indian press accounts, surveys by volunteer organizations, and U.S. government and Union Carbide documents.

This book is the result of my investigation. What I learned confirmed my belief that there was a great deal the U.S. public was not hearing about the catastrophe. In fact, since there was so much not being said that could and should have been, it was obvious that a mammoth coverup was going on, involving Union Carbide, the U.S. chemical industry, the U.S. media, and the U.S. government itself.

The Bhopal disaster deserves the fullest possible scrutiny and exposure, and I hope this book will contribute to that. It could not have been written without the help of many people in India, who were eager to assist in this effort. They were invaluable in providing information and anxious to share ideas, to suggest relevant lines of investigation, to help in translation of documents, and to introduce me to contacts and friends. In a very real way this book is theirs. I would also like to thank environmentalists and others in the U.S. who have provided valuable materials, ideas, and encouragement, as well as criticisms of early drafts.

I have chosen the word massacre to sum up what happened in Bhopal. It certainly isn't the word Union Carbide Corporation or the U.S. media are using, but I believe those reading this book will end up agreeing that there is no other way to describe accurately what took place.

Map of Bhopal and
Location of UCC Plant

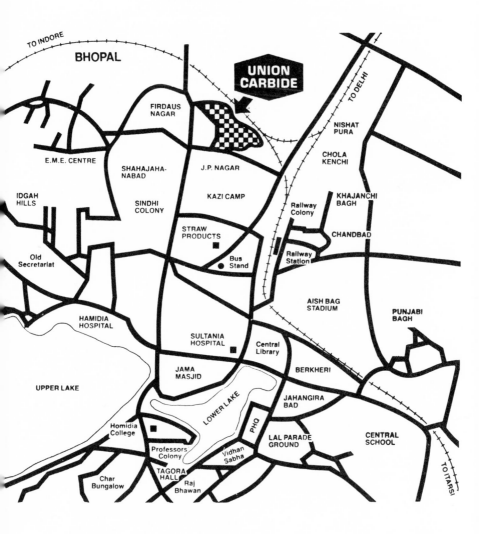

1 | The Night of Horror

Sunday, December 2, 1984 began routinely enough at the Union Carbide pesticide factory in Bhopal, India. The factory, which had been hailed by Union Carbide and local officials as an oasis of progress in this rapidly growing city of over 900,000 and as a sign that Bhopal was entering the modern era, produced carbamate pesticides from chemical intermediaries, one of which was methyl isocyanate (MIC).

The MIC production unit had been shut down for nearly two months, and that night workers were performing routine maintenance that included washing out lines linked to the plant's three MIC storage tanks. Washing began around 9:30 p.m. By about 11:00 p.m.workers became aware of an MIC leak, but they couldn't locate its source. Assumed to be the kind of "normal" leak that often occurred at the plant, little attention was paid to it. By midnight, however, there were signs that something was profoundly wrong.

The sting of MIC was getting stronger and the temperature and pressure were rapidly rising in MIC storage tank 610. When a worker investigated around 12:30 a.m., he felt the ground around the tank shake and rumble, and heard a gigantic hiss. A runaway chemical chain reaction, triggered by the entrance of water, had taken place in the tank, creating tremendous heat and pressure. Forty tons of deadly gases burst past the rupture disc, overwhelmed the plant's safety systems, and shot into the atmosphere. Most of the workers fled in panic.

Just east of the factory, in the densely packed shanty settlement of Chhola Kenchi, Ishmail Khan and his wife were sound asleep. He is in his late twenties, but despite his youth, his six days of work as a *hamal*, or load carrier – queuing up each morning to get work that would earn him five to twenty rupees a day (approximately thirteen rupees equal one dollar) – left him exhausted by the end of the week and looking forward to a Sunday of rest and sleep. His first warning that something was wrong was a burning sensation in his eyes, and a choking, gasping lack of breath. The gas had poured silently through the surrounding neighborhoods and was suddenly upon the people.

"I sleep with my mouth open," he recalled, "so I was the first to awaken, around 1:00. I was coughing and coughing; and my eyes were burning horribly. I ran outside to see what was happening, and people were running in all directions at once. I rushed back into the house to awaken my wife and brother-in-law. By then the gas hung like a thick cloud covering Chhola Kenchi. We just ran away."

Throughout the slums and shanty settlements that surround the Union Carbide plant on three sides, thousands were awakened by the suffocating, burning effects of the gas, the cries of neighbors, the clamor of running, stumbling feet, or by the howls of animals in their death throes. Some didn't wake up. They died immediately without even being able to cry for help.

Some initially thought that the burning sensation came from roasting chilis. A few thought the plant was on fire and rushed toward it to help. No one, even those living in the shadow of the factory, had been forewarned about the deadly effects of the chemicals used at the Union Carbide factory; the factory alarm was not sounded until well after the gases had burst into the atmosphere and no one received guidance from the plant; no government officials were present to direct people to safety.

"Everyone was confused," one witness said. "Mothers didn't know their children had died. Children didn't know their mothers had died. Men didn't know their whole families had died. Anyone who was left alive ran away blindly."[1] But the very cloud of gases the people of Bhopal were trying to escape was thwarting their flight. The toxic cloud was so dense and searing that people were reduced to near blindness in their rush through narrow, ill-lit alleys. Its effects became ever more suffocating, the harder one gasped for breath, the more frenzied one's flight. The deadly brew of gases burned the tissues of the eyes and lungs and attacked the nervous system. People began vomiting uncontrollably, were wracked with seizures and quickly fell dead. Others drowned in their own secretions as their lungs − ravaged by the killer gases − filled with fluid.

Some who managed to hang onto life panicked, leaving loved ones behind. Families who tried to stay together were often separated momentarily in the blinding gas and then unable to regroup. Others were simply torn apart by the stampede, like flood victims pulled apart by roaring currents. People were falling down, crashing into each other, stumbling over bricks and bodies in the mad, chaotic dash for life.

"We ran toward the railway station to try and get away," Ishmail said. "We were moving as a group, but it was shattered, people were running every which way. Before I knew what had happened my brother-in-law and wife were gone. I went back to look for them, but I fell down, I couldn't breathe. After ten minutes, I gathered all my will and forced myself to stand up again and begin running. I got a ride in a car to Ambadkar Nagar, 10 kilometers away from here. There I collapsed and was unconscious for an hour."

Soon there was a massive exodus away from the Union Carbide factory, now a fount of death, a stream of humanity tens of thousands strong − walking, running, clinging to taxis, trucks, three-wheeled autorickshaws or any other means of escape they could find. It was a current so strong it was virtually impossible to brook, one that would carry many as far as 20 kilometers from Bhopal. All told the gas spread over some 40 square kilometers, affecting 200,000 people and driving half the city out of their homes in search of safety.

Union Carbide management did not alert local authorities when the gases exploded into the atmosphere. The superintendent of police was one of the first officials to learn of the disaster.

He was called, shortly after 1:00 a.m., by some of his men who were stationed near the factory and affected by the gas. Arriving at his station around 1:30, he called the Carbide plant several times, but could get no information. At around 1:45 the additional district magistrate reached the works manager, J. Mukund, at home. "How can there be a leak at my plant," he responded, "it's been shut down." At about 3:00 a Carbide official walked into the station. There has been a leak, he told them, but it was now under control.[2]

Civil authority was virtually nonexistent. Moti Singh, one of the chief administrative officials for the city, was informed of the leak around 1:30. He then left town and later began operating from the Bairagarh police station, about six miles from Bhopal. He cited safety as the reason for leaving. The first government official reached the factory at 4:30, roughly two hours after the gas had stopped leaking. The first meeting of secretaries and department heads to coordinate the government's response took place some 40 hours after the gas leak. There were heroic efforts to save people that night, but they were mainly individual and ad hoc.

Interns and medical students at the Gandhi Medical College/ Hamidia Hospital complex in central Bhopal had been awakened, like tens of thousands of others, by the cloud of gases. They also had little idea of what had hit them and rushed away from its deadly effects. By 5:00 or 6:00 in the morning many of them had returned to Hamidia to find out what was happening and to help out if needed. Dr. Upadyaya, a resident at Hamidia, reached the hospital around 4:00 a.m. and, finding few patients there, went back to sleep. When he awoke two hours later the hospital was crammed with thousands. "People were everywhere: in the halls, on the floors, outside on the lawns, in every corner of the hospital. People and people. Most of them were lying down weeping, moaning, or crying – and they couldn't even open their eyes because of the gas. They'd lost a daughter or a son, maybe a mother or father. None of the families were complete."

Bhopal's medical facilities and doctors were quickly overwhelmed with people, suffering from gases about which they knew next to nothing. When contacted by doctors on duty, Union Carbide's chief medical officer told them MIC was a nontoxic irritant. He mentioned nothing of the possibility of other gases also being involved.[3]

Life-saving medicines and equipment were in short supply. "There were thousands of patients and we only had a few oxygen cylinders. Now whom do you give oxygen, and whom not?" recalled Dr. Ashok Gupta. "Everything was utter confusion...it was impossible to cope with this. That day nothing was clear about MIC." By the end of the first day nearly 20,000 people were treated in the 1,000-bed Hamidia Hospital alone. "We didn't even have enough space to keep the corpses," said Dr. Gupta. "We stacked them one on top of another like they were bags of wheat."

At 4:30 in the morning the first newsmen, from the English *Free Press Journal* and the Hindi *Navbharat Times*, reached the factory. Save for the plant's dispensary, "there was complete calm." They found works manager Mukund in his office. There, leaning back in his chair, hands clasped behind his head, he told them, "Our safety measures are the best in the country." He assured the reporter from the *Navbharat Times* that MIC was only an irritant, not a deadly poison. Another Carbide official said, "Nothing has happened. Can't you see us alive?" According to the *Free Press Journal*, "several dead bodies lay barely 100 yards from where he was standing,"[4] just outside the plant gates.

The chemical reaction played itself out between 2:00 and 3:00 in the morning, as the toxic cloud began to dissipate. In the next hours, as people staggered and drifted back to their homes, the full dimensions of the disaster began to be apparent. Bhopal looked like a battle zone in a chemical war. It was littered with the dead – lying in alleys, ditches, roadways, or still trapped in their huts, in the contorted positions of sudden death. They lay intermingled with the goats, cows, sheep, and other animals that had also perished. The gas cloud had devastated everything living in its path, even killing plants and turning leaves black. "People were just lying in the road like dogs and cats," Ishmail Khan recalled. One paper noted that it was easy to locate the plant from afar – vultures were circling overhead.

The survivors wandered among the carnage desperately seeking family and loved ones they had lost in the chaotic night. Some were too shocked to do anything. Ishmail had managed to get a bus back into Bhopal and then walked to his hut in Chhola

Kenchi. His wife had somehow found her way back home; Ishmail never saw his brother-in-law again. He rushed his wife to Hamidia Hospital; she died there three days later. Lines of people searching for missing relatives stretched for over a kilometer outside the city morgue. The search proved lucky for 13-year-old Nasseem Bano. While running from the gas she had fallen unconscious on a footpath. Later in the morning, still unconscious, she had been taken for dead, thrown in the back of an army truck, and taken to the morgue. Her uncle found her there the next day – barely alive.

Rows of shroud-covered bodies lined Bhopal's morgues and cemeteries. The gas had struck hardest at the poor: they lived closest to the Union Carbide plant, and few – if any – had cars or even scooters for a quick escape. Of the poor, the very young and very old – those with the least ability to resist or flee the deadly gases – fared the worst. For the next several days crematoriums and burial grounds worked around the clock. Whole families were burned on one pyre; old graves were dug up to make way for the new; several bodies were put into each grave.

The total number of dead may never be known. The Indian government's official estimate, at last count, was 1,754.[5] Popular estimates in Bhopal range from 5,000 to 10,000; most people think at least 5,000 perished. Tens of thousands who managed to survive have been afflicted with a variety of crippling aftereffects. In the weeks that followed, doctors reported finding, among other things, damage to the lungs, eyes, intestines, and nervous system. There were mounting incidences of spontaneous abortions and stillbirths. Like thousands of others, Ishmail Khan could no longer work. His legs, hands, and chest ached all the time, it was difficult for him to see in bright daylight, and he was overcome by dizziness and breathlessness after even short spurts of strenuous activity.

People continue to die from the effects of the gassing. Estimates of the number severely debilitated run as high as 60,000. And one can only speculate on what the long-term effects of such a massive exposure to toxins will be. All in all it was the worst industrial disaster in history.

2 | Design for Disaster

Few would deny that the lives of hundreds of millions in the underdeveloped countries consist daily of unrelieved poverty and misery, even though in the industrialized countries of the West this is usually not considered a newsworthy subject. But when this "normal" misery becomes concentrated and explodes – as in the incineration of hundreds in a natural gas inferno in San Juan Ixhuatepec, Mexico; the starvation deaths of millions in Ethiopia and other parts of Africa; or the drowning of untold numbers in Bangladesh – the names of these hitherto "remote" places and their stories flash fleetingly across the headlines and television screens before returning to obscurity. Such events generally are portrayed as an unavoidable calamity: the basic stuff of life, and death, in the Third World. If explanations are advanced at all, they obscure rather than focus on the underlying economic and social forces that cause these disasters. The horror of Bhopal is one such example, and we must answer the fundamental questions: why did it happen and who was responsible?

Union Carbide reacted to the disaster in Bhopal as if it were a bolt from the blue. It was characterized as "a unique combination

17

of unusual events,"[1] an aberration for a corporation where "safety is a critical element in all our operations" and is rigorously applied in whatever corner of the globe Union Carbide operates in.[2] "Our safety standards in the U.S. are identical to those in India or Brazil or someplace else," Union Carbide Chairman Warren Anderson stated. "Same equipment, same design, same everything."[3]

The disaster occurred, according to Union Carbide's "Bhopal Methyl Isocyanate Incident Investigation Team Report" of March 20, 1985, due to "the deliberate or inadvertent introduction" of water into MIC tank 610 (i.e., the question of possible sabotage is raised), and a series of actions "not in compliance with standard operating procedures."[4] The company emphasized that the catastrophe had not exposed faults in "the process chemistry, the process design and engineering, and the safeguards built into the system."[5]

Union Carbide argued that it neither knew about nor was responsible for these procedural violations, and that responsibility for the disaster rested entirely on the shoulders of its Indian subsidiary, the Bhopal employees in particular. "You can't run a $9 or $10 billion corporation all out of Danbury," Warren Anderson said; the lines of communication "were broken at the Bhopal plant."[6] "Compliance with these procedures is the responsibility of operating plant personnel," Anderson summed up.[7]

Much more is at stake here than the question of who has ultimate responsibility for a particular factory, and the related problem of costly liability. In the wake of the Bhopal disaster, many sharp questions have been raised not only about Union Carbide's practices in India, but more generally the practices of foreign capital in all the underdeveloped countries. Thus the argument that design and attention to safety are identical at all Union Carbide facilities, whether in the U.S. or in the Third World, and that the main problem in Bhopal was the failure of local management and employees to follow company procedures, is linked by Carbide officials to the more fundamental assessment that countries like India are simply unable to handle the complex, "state-of-the-art" technology that companies like Union Carbide provide.

This problem of technological backwardness was exacerbated, the argument continues, by nationalist-inspired Indian government regulations which place a large degree of control of foreign-owned operations in Indian hands. "In many countries outside the industrialized West, the cultural background or basic educational level simply cannot support the ongoing operation of sophisticated technologies," Union Carbide writes in the "After Bhopal" essay in its 1984 annual report. "And it is a fact that in some countries, local laws require that new facilities be built and operated with local labor or materials, or that they be managed or staffed exclusively by nationals of the host country."[8]

Overwhelmingly, the U.S. media advanced the same analysis. An expert told the *Wall Street Journal*, "We are thrusting 20th century technology into countries that aren't ready to deal with it."[9] *Chemical and Engineering News* writes that "absent too often is a 'safety mentality,' a 'mechanical' sense of things required for that safety infrastructure," and concludes, "It is the bitter fruit of indigenization, the consensus now reads, that was basically to blame for the Bhopal disaster."[10]

The main U.S. media analysis of the disaster appeared in a *New York Times* series between January 28 and February 3, 1985. This was somewhat broader than Union Carbide's report on the particulars of the accident, mentioning contributory factors such as "design flaws" and "economy measures that endangered safety," as well as leaving open the question of who controlled the Bhopal operation. But the *New York Times* analysis is basically complementary to Union Carbide's because it focuses principally on ten procedural violations its investigation turned up.

More importantly, the *New York Times* fundamentally agrees on the deeper causes and lessons of the disaster. The article, "Disaster in Bhopal: Where Does Blame Lie?" deals almost solely with India's lax environmental regulations. The concluding article, "The Disaster in Bhopal: Lessons for the Future," strongly emphasizes India's low educational and technical level. "Hazardous facilities often pose added risks in developing nations, where skilled labor and public understanding are often lacking," the article declares.[11]

The underlying thrust of these analyses is that multinational corporations are essentially a force for world progress — exemplified in India by rising food production stimulated by companies like Union Carbide and its pesticide plant in Bhopal. Disasters like the one in Bhopal are tragic but also more or less inevitable – the price of progress as it were. "History teaches that there is no avoiding that hazard [of technology], and no point in trying," *Time* magazine editorialized; "one only trusts that the gods in the machines will give a good deal more than they take away."[12] Furthermore, when such disasters do occur, the problem resides ultimately in the Third World's inability to absorb these technological and other benefits, and in its short-sighted insistence on a degree of self-reliance. In short, the Bhopal catastrophe and other such industrial horrors in the Third World are caused, at root, by the victims themselves.

My own investigation and analysis of the Bhopal disaster and the circumstances surrounding it leads to a much different conclusion. First, the assertions of Union Carbide, the U.S. chemical industry, and the U.S. media amount to a patchwork of blatant omissions, outright lies, and an incredibly narrow, chauvinist rendering of events. Second, while procedural violations and technological backwardness in India certainly are components of the disaster, its root causes are to be found not there, but in the overall relationship between the industrialized or "advanced" countries and the Third World, a relationship characterized by the domination of the former over the latter. Third, this domination of foreign capital provides the critical context for understanding the statements and actions of the various principal forces and individuals who took the stage in this unprecedented disaster.

The Accident

Union Carbide Corporation (UCC), with headquarters in Danbury, Connecticut, is the 35th largest industrial company in the U.S. and operates plants in 38 countries,* manufacturing a wide range of products, from consumer goods to industrial chemicals to powerful pesticides. Of UCC's 1984 assets of $11 billion and sales of $9.5 billion, over 14 percent derived from holdings in

---

*Union Carbide's far-flung holdings include nine plants in the Union of South Africa.

Asia, Africa, the Middle East, and Latin America, and 21.6 percent of its $323 million in profits derived from those operations.[13]

UCC operates in India through its subsidiary, Union Carbide of India Limited (UCIL), of which it owns 50.9 percent of the stock (the remaining stock is owned by Indian investors). Union Carbide has been doing business in India since 1905, and by 1983 UCIL had grown into one of India's 40 largest industrial concerns,[14] with 14 plants manufacturing batteries, chemicals, pesticides, and other products. In 1983 it had sales of $202 million and profits of $8.8 million.[15] In 1969 it opened its pesticide plant in Bhopal, the capital of the state of Madhya Pradesh in central India. Originally a formulation plant to mix and package pesticides imported from the U.S., it was expanded and by 1980 manufactured carbamate pesticides, trade-named "Sevin" and "Temik," from chemical intermediaries mostly produced on site.*

In the MIC production unit, carbon monoxide, manufactured in the plant, is first reacted with chlorine, which is transported in, to form phosgene. Phosgene is then combined with mono-methylamine to form methyl isocyanate (MIC). MIC is stored in three 15,000-gallon tanks, designated 610, 611, and 619. It is transferred as needed to the Sevin or Temik units, where it is reacted with alpha napthol to produce the pesticides.

Chlorine, phosgene, monomethylamine, and MIC are all deadly. Union Carbide's 1976 manual, "Methyl Isocyanate," begins by stating that MIC is "reactive, toxic, volatile, and flammable." It calls it a "hazardous material by all means of contact," a "poison by inhalation," and an "oral and contact poison." MIC's threshold limit value, how much a worker supposedly can breathe safely in eight hours, is .02 parts per million, making it five times more deadly, by this measure, than phosgene, the chemical weapon used with such devastating effect in World War 1.

This manual warns that MIC is so volatile that stringent precautions are needed in handling it, and even warn that various contaminants, including water, chlorine, and iron, can trigger

---

*The plant was closed shortly following the disaster, and in July 1985 the Madhya Pradesh government refused to renew Union Carbide's operating license. Union Carbide then closed down the plant permanently that same month.

deadly reactions. "Methyl isocyanate can undergo a 'runaway' reaction if contaminated," it states. "A vapor cloud constitutes hazards from the standpoint of ignition (a 'fireball' could result) and toxicity."[16]

On the night of December 2, the MIC production unit had been shut down for six weeks due to an oversupply of carbamate pesticides, and workers were performing routine maintenance on the unit.

At about 9:30 p.m. a relatively new worker, on instructions from a new supervisor, began flushing with water the lines of four process filters which were part of the MIC production unit. These lines are connected to another pipeline, the relief valve vent header (RVVH), which is designed to carry toxic gases escaping from the MIC tanks in the event of a pressure buildup. The RVVH runs between the MIC tanks and the vent gas scrubber (VGS), which is designed to neutralize toxic gases.

According to *Business India* magazine, the worker did close a valve designed to isolate the pipelines which were being washed, from the RVVH. But he didn't insert a slip blind (a metal disc used to seal pipeline valves) to insure that water wouldn't leak through the valve. Further, while four bleeder valves were opened to allow water to flow out of the pipelines, two of them were totally clogged and the other two were only partially open. The washing reportedly was stopped temporarily when workers noticed that water wasn't flowing freely out of the bleeder valves, but it was resumed shortly thereafter on the supervisor's instructions, without the blockage being removed.[17]

With no outlet, water pressure built up, and water forced its way past the closed isolation valve – valves were notoriously leaky at the plant – and into the RVVH. Normally water still couldn't enter the MIC tanks because there are a number of closed valves between the RVVH and the tanks. In addition, the rupture disc, between the MIC tanks and the RVVH, only opens under pressure from the MIC tanks and is unidirectional – from the tanks outward.

But a recently installed pipe, or jumper line, provided another route for water to enter the MIC tanks. The jumper line ran between the RVVH and the process vent header (PVH), another pipeline leading from the MIC tanks to the vent gas scrubber. The function of the PVH is similar but not identical to that of the RVVH. The PVH carries gases released while the MIC tanks are being pressurized with nitrogen in order to transfer MIC to the pesticide production unit. In May of 1984, the jumper line had been installed in order to simplify maintenance procedures, and in lieu of a more expensive backup line for the vent headers. If either the PVH or the RVVH were undergoing repairs, the toxic gases it normally carried to the vent gas scrubber could now be channeled, via the jumper line, through whichever of the two vent headers was operating.*

On December 2, repairs were in progress on the process vent header, and the jumper line had been opened up. There was also a leak in the valves and piping leading to the MIC tank. For the past week, workers had been in the process of starting up the Sevin unit, which had also been shut down. To transfer MIC from the storage tanks into the Sevin unit to begin pesticide production, the MIC tanks must be pressurized with liquid nitrogen. Yet for a week prior to December 2, workers had been unable to pressurize tank 610; apparently one of the valves sealing the tank was faulty, allowing nitrogen to leak out. On December 2, the leak had been neither found nor repaired.

The open jumper line provided a route for the water into the PVH, and the faulty valve that had prevented the pressurization of tank 610 then allowed water to pass from the PVH into tank 610.[19]

By itself, the entry of water into tank 610 may not have been catastrophic. But other conditions in this tank made it ripe for disaster. The tank contained between 11,290 and 13,000 gallons (more than 90,000 pounds) of MIC, making it between 75 and 87 percent full.[20] Union Carbide manuals state that MIC tanks should never be over 50 to 60 percent full for safety reasons — the extra space can be used to dilute the MIC or absorb heat in the event of a runaway reaction.[21] Meanwhile, tank 619, which was

---

*The existence of this jumper line has been substantiated by India's Central Bureau of Investigation (CBI), Indian environmentalists, journalists who investigated the disaster, and by an international delegation from several labor unions, whose report was published on August 1, 1985. On that same day, Union Carbide confirmed the existence of the jumper line; it had not mentioned this critical fact in its March 20 report.[18]

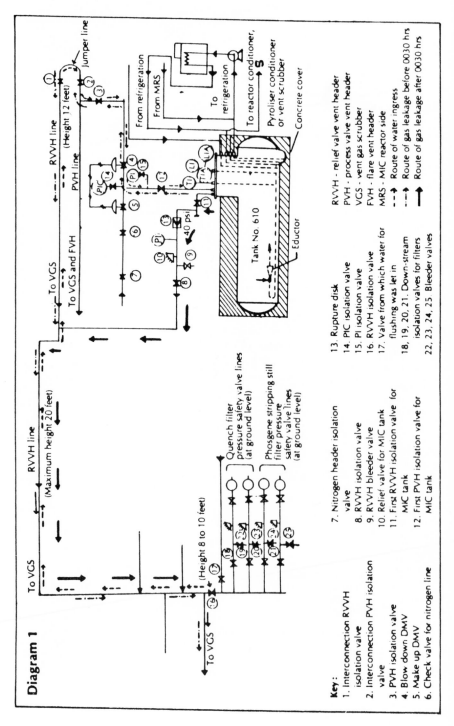

Diagram 1

Key:
1. Interconnection RVVH isolation valve
2. Interconnection PVH isolation valve
3. PVH isolation valve
4. Blow down DMV
5. Make up DMV
6. Check valve for nitrogen line
7. Nitrogen header isolation valve
8. RVVH isolation valve
9. RVVH bleeder valve
10. Relief valve for MIC tank
11. First RVVH isolation valve for MIC tank
12. First PVH isolation valve for MIC tank
13. Rupture disk
14. PIC isolation valve
15. PI isolation valve
16. RVVH isolation valve
17. Valve from which water for flushing was let in
18, 19, 20, 21. Down-stream isolation valves for filters
22, 23, 24, 25 Bleeder valves

RVVH - relief valve vent header
PVH - process valve vent header
VGS - vent gas scrubber
FVH - flare vent header
MRS - MIC reactor side

- - → Route of water ingress
- - -→ Route of gas leakage before 0030 hrs
——→ Route of gas leakage after 0030 hrs

Labels within diagram:
Jumper line
RVVH line
PVH line
(Height 12 feet)
To VGS
To VGS and FVH
RVVH line
(Maximum height 20 feet)
To VGS
(Height 8 to 10 feet)
To VGS
Quench filter pressure safety valve lines (at ground level)
Phosgene stripping still filter pressure safety valve lines (at ground level)
From refrigeration
From MRS
To refrigeration
To reactor conditioner, S
Pyroliser conditioner or vent scrubber
Concrete cover
Tank No. 610
Eductor
40 psi

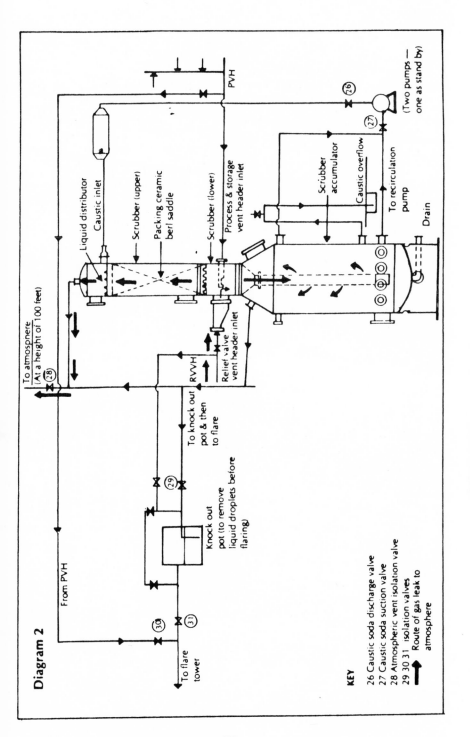

Diagram 2

Liquid distributor
Caustic inlet
Scrubber (upper)
Packing ceramic berl saddle
Scrubber (lower)
Process & storage vent header inlet

Scrubber accumulator
Caustic overflow
To recirculation pump
Drain

(Two pumps — one as stand by)

To atmosphere (At a height of 100 feet)

RVVH
Relief valve vent header inlet

To knock out pot & then to flare

PVH

Knock out pot (to remove liquid droplets before flaring)

From PVH

To flare tower

KEY

26 Caustic soda discharge valve
27 Caustic soda suction valve
28 Atmospheric vent isolation valve
29 30 31 isolation valves
Route of gas leak to atmosphere

25

supposed to be kept empty to serve as an emergency dump tank for contaminated MIC, contained 2,400 pounds of MIC.[22]

The MIC in tank 610 also contained thirty-two times more chloroform, which is used as a solvent in the MIC manufacturing process, than the normal level of 0.5 percent.[23] Carbide publications warn that chlorine compounds can react with MIC as well as the stainless steel walls of MIC storage tanks to produce heat, liberate metal ions, and contribute to a runaway chain reaction.*[24] But workers weren't aware that tank 610 was contaminated; it hadn't been sampled since late October when the MIC unit was last in operation (and perhaps hadn't been accurately sampled then).[25]

Finally, the temperature in the tank was above safe limits. Keeping MIC cool through refrigeration is a crucial safety precaution because it makes the chemical much less reactive, and slows down reactions should a tank be contaminated, giving operators more time to deal with the situation. But, as an economy measure, the refrigeration unit at Bhopal had been shut down for over five months. On December 2, tank temperatures ranged between 15 and 20 degrees C. instead of the preferred 0 to 5 degrees C.[26]

The water entering tank 610 reacted with the MIC, creating intense heat. The combination of heat, water, and excess chloroform led to corrosion of the stainless steel walls of the tank, freeing iron. The iron catalyzed other exothermic reactions† involving MIC, reaccelerating the whole process. This chain reaction went on for nearly three hours – from sometime after 9:30 p.m. to around 12:30 a.m. It ultimately involved most of the 90,000 pounds of MIC in the tank and generated enormous heat and pressure.

During this three-hour period, the workers in the plant were unaware that anything out of the ordinary was taking place. Tank 610 has one temperature alarm, which also sounds in the control room. It never went off that night, because it hadn't been reset to sound above the already elevated tank temperature of 15 to 20

---

*A runaway chemical chain reaction is a series of chemical reactions in which the products of each reaction activate additional molecules of the reactants, thus causing new reactions.

†A chemical change in which there is a liberation of heat, as in combustion.

degrees C. The tank temperature wasn't recorded in plant logs either; thus, when the third shift came on duty at 10:45 p.m., the operators would not be aware that it was rising.[27]

The tank also has a pressure indicator. At around 10:30, pressure in tank 610 stood at 2 psig (pounds per square inch above atmospheric pressure). At 11:00, the new operator noticed that it was 10 psig. However, it is unclear if he had been informed of the earlier reading and was aware of the rapid rise. Carbide claimed that normal tank pressures range between 2 and 25 psig so he thought nothing of it. In any case, he did nothing about it.[28]

Also around 11:00, workers felt the tearing sting of MIC and realized there was a leak. But no one could find its source. The shift supervisor was reportedly told of the leak around 11:45. He said he would deal with it after the tea break, scheduled at 12:15.[29]

As tea ended, another MIC leak was reported and operators noticed the pressure in tank 610 had shot up to 30 psig, then quickly to 55 psig – the maximum gauge reading. An operator ran to the tank to investigate, heard it rumbling, and saw the concrete above it cracking. By this time temperatures in the tank had shot up past 200 degrees C.; pressures had risen from 2 psig to over 180 psig. A deadly brew of MIC and other toxic chemicals burst past the tank's rupture disc – set at 40 psig – shot through the relief valve vent header, past the vent gas scrubber, and into the atmosphere.[30]

At this late hour, when the workers finally realized the enormity of the crisis, they tried vainly to activate the plant's safety systems. The vent gas scrubber, the plant's main line of defense against escaping gas, had been on "standby," because it was felt it was not needed when MIC was only being stored, not produced. It was turned on, sometime after 12:30, but it is unclear whether it ever became operative. It is clear that it had little impact on the massive leak. Workers considered turning on the plant's flare tower, a safety device designed to burn off escaping toxins. Then they realized that a section of pipe, linking it to the VGS and the MIC tanks, had been removed for maintenance work. They also considered dumping the contaminated MIC into tank 619 which was supposed to be used as a spare; but its gauge incorrectly read that it was 22 percent full and they feared this would spread the problem rather than contain it.[31] The workers then tried to douse the leak with water. The spray reached 100 feet into the air; the gas was escaping from a stack roughly 120 feet in the air.[32]

By the time the reaction had dissipated, about two hours later, Union Carbide estimates that of the 90,000 pounds of MIC in tank 610, 54,000 pounds of unreacted MIC and 26,000 pounds of "reaction products" blasted into the atmosphere over Bhopal.*[33]

The Question of Design

Since Union Carbide Corporation was responsible for the basic design of the Bhopal plant, the contention that this design is sound – is identical to its other MIC production facility at Institute, West Virginia, and similar plants in the industrialized world, and therefore didn't contribute to the disaster – is central to the claim that the roots of the catastrophe in Bhopal lie in India's inability to handle complex technology, and that direct responsibility for what happened lies with the Indian subsidiary. This contention is wrong in all respects.

A principle of safe industrial design is that one does not guard merely against the most predictable, routine types of accidents. Rather, one tries to anticipate the worst that could happen, even if unlikely, and not only guard against it, but prepare to contain it if the worst does take place. "We try to design safety into our systems," says Geraldine Cox, the vice president and technical director of the Chemical Manufacturers Association. "It's a process of calculating extremes, then designing beyond that."[34]

Union Carbide describes its design and safety practices in similar terms. "Safety is a critical element in all our operations," says Jackson Browning, Carbide's director of health, safety, and environmental affairs. "It is one of our primary considerations, from the very beginning, for assessing which method and/or process is to be employed in making a product." He also says that Carbide has an "ongoing system of operation safety surveys," and that one of its purposes is "to find fault, to examine worst case

---

*The other 10,000 pounds never left tank 610.

situations."[35]

All this naturally should go ten times over for a plant manu-facturing and processing chemicals such as MIC, so dangerous that Union Carbide's own publications warn repeatedly of its ex-tremely toxic and reactive nature. But despite the well-known danger of MIC and all the safety talk in Union Carbide manuals, the process employed to manufacture carbamate pesticides at both its Institute and Bhopal plants has by no means been the safest one possible. Neither plant's safety systems were designed to meet extremes or cope with worst case situations, with those at the Bhopal plant inferior to those at Institute. And at the Bhopal plant, instrumentation and control devices, crucial for even routine safety, were inadequate and less extensive than those at Institute. In short, neither Bhopal nor Institute was designed with safety as the primary consideration, but the situation was significantly worse in Bhopal.

The Bhopal plant's faulty design put in place the elements of a catastrophe. Its flaws were one key reason why workers didn't realize that there was anything wrong for three hours after trou-ble began, couldn't locate the problem when its first signs ap-peared, couldn't contain the chemical chain reaction when they realized what was happening, and couldn't neutralize the escap-ing poison when it began pouring into the atmosphere over Bhopal. In sum, a major problem in Bhopal was not more technology than the employees could handle, but an abysmal, dangerous lack of it.

Union Carbide has increasingly tried to distance itself from responsibility for the design of the Bhopal plant and place the onus for its flaws on UCIL. The corporation's July 31, 1985 affi-davit to dismiss charges filed against it in U.S. courts states, "Union Carbide transferred certain process design packages to UCIL for the Bhopal Plant. However, the blueprints and detail design plans for the Bhopal Plant were prepared entirely in India...Union Carbide does not have sets of the detail design drawings or the blueprints of the Plant as it was finally built."[36]

Union Carbide may have provided a "design package," while detailed design and construction were carried out in India, but the implication here, that Union Carbide neither oversaw the design of its Bhopal plant nor knew how it was finally built, is totally false. According to former Union Carbide of India's managing director, Edward A. Munoz, a corporate engineering group in South Charleston, West Virginia, was "assigned primary responsibility for engineering and construction of the Bhopal MIC unit. The group performed the design report which contained all of the flow diagrams, material and energy balances, operating manuals and all other necessary information to base mechanical design, erection, start-up and operation of the MIC manufacturing and storage facilities." The engineering group oversaw and continuously monitored the design and construction of the MIC plant.[37]

Further, the design flaws at the Bhopal plant were not a matter of misplaced nuts and bolts, i.e., deviations from an essentially sound plan. Rather, as we shall examine, some were fundamental to the basic process chosen by UCC to produce MIC, and also exist at its Institute plant. Others concerned the overall capacities of key pieces of equipment, which certainly would – or should – have been specified in whatever "design package" Union Carbide sent to UCIL. Many of the precise details of Bhopal's flawed design could also have been specified in UCC's design package, as the technology needed to manufacture MIC-based pesticides is complex, and that technology was not developed and fundamentally controlled by UCIL or an Indian engineering firm, but by UCC.*[38]

To begin with, MIC can be made without using the dangerous phosgene and chlorine, by employing instead the nontoxic chemicals dimethyl urea and diphenylcarbonate, as is done, for example, at the Bayer plant in West Germany.[40] It is also possible to make carbamate pesticides by reacting phosgene with alpha napthol, without using MIC at all. While phosgene is also deadly, its threshold limit value is much higher than that of MIC, and in this process it is generally not stored but converted directly into

---

*Significantly, Union Carbide's July 31 affidavit also contains a fall-back position on the issue of plant design. It states that even if the allegation of defective design is true, "the cases should still be dismissed. . . . In case after case, allegations that products were defectively designed in the United States have been held insufficient to defeat motions to dismiss on grounds of *forum non conveniens*."[39] (*Forum non conveniens* is Union Carbide's argument that the Bhopal cases should be heard in India.)

pesticide. Carbide chose the more dangerous MIC method because it is more "efficient": the process involving MIC produces a purer grade of pesticide, with fewer waste products and less corrosion of pipelines and equipment, and it can also be used to produce a variety of pesticides.[41]

This choice of method was compounded by the decision to store large amounts of MIC in bulk storage tanks rather than in small containers, or processing the MIC as it was produced, without storage. Union Carbide publications acknowledge that bulk storage of MIC heightens the danger of both leakage and contamination.[42] And, as Bhopal so grimly demonstrated, it greatly magnifies the consequences of an accident should one take place.

Because of these potential dangers, known long before December 2, 1984, a number of plants that produce MIC store it only in small quantities or use it as it is produced. At Bayer's MIC plant in Dormagen, West Germany, on the average only 10 tons in four separate tanks can be stored – less than one-tenth of the capacity of the MIC storage tanks in Bhopal.[43] The pesticide plant currently being built by Dupont in LaPorte, Texas is designed to process MIC as it is produced. A similar process is used by Mitsubishi in Japan.[44]

Was the decision to store MIC in bulk at the Bhopal plant made by Indians who didn't comprehend the dangers of modern chemical technology? According to Edward A. Munoz, when the plant was being designed he and the UCIL management argued that "only token storage was necessary, preferably in small individual containers based on both economic and safety considerations." They were overruled by the corporate engineering group in the U.S., which insisted upon large bulk storage tanks patterned on those at Carbide's MIC plant in Institute, which has three 14,000-gallon above-ground tanks and three 30,000-gallon underground storage tanks.[45]

The critical element in this decision, as in the decision to use the more dangerous method of making MIC, again proved to be production efficiency. If the production process called for only token storage or the immediate conversion of MIC into carbamates, then any breakdown in the MIC production unit would halt production of Sevin. Storing large quantities of MIC was

Union Carbide's solution to this potential production bottleneck: MIC could be accumulated while its production was running smoothly, assuring that an adequate supply of the chemical was on hand whenever needed to produce carbamate pesticides.[46] Also, MIC produced at Union Carbide's Institute plant is wholesaled to other pesticide manufacturers. It is reasonable to infer that Union Carbide may also have insisted on bulk storage in Bhopal because it was planning to wholesale large amounts of MIC from there too, in what it predicted would be a rapidly growing Indian pesticide market. (Before the disaster, UCIL was already wholesaling some MIC produced in Bhopal to other pesticide manufacturers.)[47]

In addition to the questions of method of production and storage, the safe design of a plant manufacturing deadly chemicals necessitates, among other things, extensive instrumentation to monitor and control the production process, and a high level of redundancy of the various systems involved. If one system breaks down, a backup system can take its place. And all of this must be designed to stand up under "worst case situations."

What was the situation at the Bhopal plant? Praful Bidwai, a chemical engineer and journalist for the *Times of India*, studied the plant following the disaster. He wrote that the design of key pieces of equipment was based on "either absurd or extravagantly optimistic assumptions," rather than the worst case analysis that should guide safe design. The Carbide plant "appears . . . to have low rates of redundancy — or none at all — in some of its crucial components," he wrote, and few gauges and indicators. He continued:

> In at least 15 different vital positions in diverse parts of the carbon monoxide-phosgene-MIC complex, there are only indicators of temperatures and flows, where there should be recorders as well, which maintain a permanent chronicle of the behavior of critical parameters. . . In the MIC plant as a whole, there are only eight "interlocks" or shutdown devices. . . whereas, according to safety engineers, there should be three times as many. . . . As if this were not bad enough, the interconnections between the instruments in the control room and those placed in the field and the plant are incredibly primitive and highly unsatisfactory.[48]

One crucial type of equipment absent in the Bhopal plant was gas detectors, capable of sensing and locating toxic leaks. At Union Carbide's Bezier, France plant, the air in the warehouse where MIC is stored is automatically monitored by sensors that measure the air content in hundredths of a part per million, and can also trigger alarms causing the whole warehouse to be flooded with water at the rate of 80,000 gallons per hour.[49] According to a recent report by the U.S. Occupational Safety and Health Administration (OSHA), Union Carbide's Institute plant has a "toxic gas alarm system which identifies precise locations of releases."[50]

In Bhopal the workers were the leak detectors: "If odor or eye irritation is not detected," the MIC unit's "Operating Manual" reads, "the MIC is not present."[51] This was Union Carbide's method in Bhopal even though the minimum detection level of MIC is 20 times higher than what is safe to breathe in an eight-hour day,[52] and despite declarations in other Carbide publications that the tear gas effect of MIC can't be relied upon to warn employees of leaks.[53]

The inadequacy of instrumentation and controls at the Bhopal plant was known to corporate headquarters in Danbury; the company's own inspectors said so following a May 1982 inspection of the Bhopal plant. "The plant relies heavily on manual control and checking of levels," the report to headquarters stated.[54] After the disaster, C.S. Tyson, the leader of the Union Carbide team that performed the 1982 inspection, told the *New York Times*, "It is an entirely different setup, the demand is on the human out there." Safety systems were manually operated in Bhopal, while they are automatic at the Carbide plant in Institute, he said. The whole plant was not "up to American standards," Tyson concluded.[55]

Interesting, in light of Chairman Anderson's claim: "same equipment, same design, same everything." And it was these major instrumentation and control shortcomings − not minor instrument flaws, procedural violations, or ignorance of supposedly sophisticated technology − that were a major reason why workers didn't realize what was taking place for three hours after the deadly chain reaction began; why they weren't able to locate and control the leaking MIC for one and one-half hours after they smelled it; and why those plant safety systems that were operative had to be turned on manually after the gases had burst into the atmosphere.

But while these shortcomings were bad enough, an even more serious design failure involved the plant's key safety systems, employed to neutralize escaping gases. Rather than being designed to handle extremes, they were capable of handling only minor leaks, and had nowhere near the capacity to deal with the kind of massive runaway reaction that occurred on December 2-3. The overall capacities of these pieces of safety equipment were certainly part of UCC's design package. Ironically, the only reason that the inadequacy of the two main systems – the vent gas scrubber and the flare tower – wasn't fully evident on the night of the disaster was that they were both turned off.

The vent gas scrubber (VGS), designed to chemically neutralize any escaping toxins with a caustic soda solution, is ostensibly the heart of the safety systems. Bhopal's operating manual states that its normal feed rate is 190 pounds per hour at 35 degrees C., and warns that "high pressure in the vent scrubber" is a process "upset," whose solution is to "check for the source of the release and rectify." In the early morning hours of December 3, gas poured through the scrubber at a rate of more than 40,000 pounds per hour, 200 times the normal rate, at temperatures exceeding 200 degrees C. The scrubber's maximum allowable working pressure is 15 psig. On the night of the disaster, pressures averaged 180 psig during the two hours the gases vented into the air.[56]

The flare tower is designed to burn off any gases the scrubber doesn't neutralize. It too would have been utterly useless even if it had been working on December 2. It is designed to handle only small quantities of MIC, perhaps a few hundred liters an hour. The piping to the flare tower is also much too small to handle a large flow of gas, and Bhopal's safety director admitted that had the workers tried to channel the escaping gases to the flare, they would have "overwhelmed the system and something would have given way somewhere else."[57] If workers had tried to light it while massive quantities of inflammable gases were rushing through, works manager Mukund figured that it "would have created a massive explosion and the flare tower would have collapsed."[58]

As a final line of defense, a series of water sprays is designed to douse and render escaping gas harmless. Union Carbide's 1982 safety inspection report recommended to U.S. headquarters that more powerful water sprays be installed. This recommendation was never implemented.[59] On the night of the disaster, workers did turn on the water spray, but it didn't reach the escaping gas.

None of the design problems enumerated here were mentioned in Union Carbide's self-proclaimed "exhaustive" March 20 report on Bhopal. But even as it insisted that the design was safe and didn't contribute to the disaster, the corporation's own actions at Institute − which was already safer than Bhopal − showed it knew otherwise. Before restarting MIC production at that plant, which was shut down immediately after the Bhopal disaster, Union Carbide invested $5 million in new safety devices in at least a dozen different areas of the plant. Many of these were precisely those areas where poor design laid the groundwork for the catastrophe in Bhopal. The capacity of the vent gas scrubber was increased by 2.5 times and larger vent headers connecting it to the MIC process unit were built.[60] Improvements were made on the flare tower. The company also "added a rate-of-rise temperature monitor and other instrumentation to insure earlier warning of any temperature rise in the storage tank," and a "computerized vapor emission tracking and warning system for the entire plant."[61]

Of course, the dangerous gas leak at the Institute plant on August 11, 1985 − a few short months after Union Carbide officials declared that "It can't happen here!" − dramatically demonstrated that these changes by no means had made Institute a safe operation.[62] The leak was triggered when steam was mistakenly piped into a jacket surrounding the bottom two-thirds of a storage tank containing a mixture of aldicarb oxime − which is combined with MIC from another tank to make aldicarb, the active ingredient in Temik − and methylene chloride, a solvent. The steam pushed up the temperature and pressures − something the operators apparently did not know about since they hadn't programmed their computer to display such changes − and eventually caused the chemicals to burst through the gaskets that seal pipelines leading out of the tank.

The safety systems then didn't work properly once the leak

had taken place. The escaping gases were not vented to the scrubbers and flares; water sprays were not powerful enough to neutralize the escaping toxins; and the newly installed computerized vapor emission tracking system predicted that the cloud of fumes would remain over the plant, so the plant's alarm was not immediately sounded. Instead, the cloud drifted over the city of Institute and 135 people had to be hospitalized. It was later reported that the computer system hadn't even been programmed to deal with leaks of the particular chemicals involved in the accident. All this underscores Union Carbide Corporation's responsibility for the design flaws at Bhopal as well.[63]

Why were these plants, Bhopal's in particular, so badly designed and lacking in adequate technology? Because paramount in Union Carbide Corporation's designing of the plants were not considerations of safety and guarding against worst case situations, but cost-cutting and profitability. Safety measures can account for between 15 and 30 percent of a new chemical plant's overall design cost – between $3 and $6 million in the case of Bhopal's $20 million plant.[64]

Also, during the past decade, when the economies of the industrialized countries have confronted serious difficulties, particularly in the most heavily industrialized sectors, the trend has been to cut back even further in safety equipment. U.S. business spending on domestic pollution control equipment, for example, has declined from 5.6 percent of capital spending in 1976 to 3 percent in 1984 and 2.7 percent in 1985.[65] Recent budgetary and other cutbacks of OSHA and the Environmental Protection Agency (EPA) – which were hardly paragons of safety and environmental monitoring and regulating to begin with – reflect the same underlying economic forces at work.

Such cost-cutting practices have made chemical plants in the U.S. and the other highly industrialized countries unsafe, as was dramatically illustrated by the massive dioxin leak which hospitalized hundreds in Seveso, Italy in 1976, and by the August 11, 1985 leak at Union Carbide's Institute plant as well. Although U.S. chemical makers have repeatedly insisted that their industry is the "safest in the world,"* a recently completed congressional

---

*In terms of "lost-time accidents," i.e., limbs lost and bones crushed, the chemical

survey of eighty-six major U.S. chemical companies found that more than sixty-two million pounds of toxic chemicals were being released every year from 302 U.S. plants.[66] Since 1980, there have been sixty-one MIC leaks at Carbide's Institute plant which have escaped the premises, and another 107 within the plant.[67]

In West Virginia's Kanawha Valley, the site of the Institute plant and a number of other chemical factories, over 676 tons of known carcinogens and 10,000 tons of other chemicals are discharged into the air every year. Studies have found that cancer rates in the Valley are 25 percent above the national average.[68]

But the situation is much worse in the underdeveloped countries. There, capital strives for higher rates of return on investments − superprofits which are critical to the overall functioning of the economies of the industrialized countries − and even less capital is generally invested by the imperialists in safety. Foreign capital generally doesn't operate under the same political constraints existing in the home countries, where some environmental reforms have been granted, and safety regulations are even more minimal and damage suits more rare than in the industrialized world. In fact, avoiding safety-related costs is one of the allures of doing business in the Third World, and U.S. industry routinely exports deadly processes and products, often banned in the domestic markets, to these countries. As one U.S. government official put it, "Once you decide that U.S. firms have to respect U.S. standards when operating abroad, you really change the whole ballgame."[69]

The differences between Union Carbide's Institute plant − even before the above-mentioned $5 million in safety improvements − and the factory at Bhopal, which made the latter much more dangerous, are an illustration. Carbide has argued that "safety devices, including flares, scrubbers, and cooling systems are part of both the Bhopal and Institute plants," as if these devices were identical.[70] But at Institute there is not only a scrubber for normal leaks as in Bhopal, but also an emergency scrub-

---

industry may well be one of the world's safest, largely because there are relatively few workers in this capital-intensive industry, and little of the kind of limb-crushing, life-devouring machinery used, for example, in coal mines or foundries. But in terms of the danger of long-term effects and catastrophic accidents, the picture is much different.

ber that is much larger. Carbide says that the vent gas scrubber at Institute has a top capacity of 60,000 pounds an hour.[71] Compare this with the scrubber at Bhopal, which has a normal feed rate of 190 pounds an hour and is "upset" by "high pressure." According to the EPA, at Institute "the flare tower has two pilot lights, igniter, and boost gas to ensure that any MIC will be incinerated. All these devices are automatically controlled with manual backup controls." The Bhopal operating manual describes the flare tower there as having a single pilot flame and no boost gas. All the safety devices in Bhopal were manually operated.[72]

The Institute plant also has larger emergency dump tanks and systems, relative to the size of its storage tanks, than Bhopal did. While all three MIC tanks are identical in size in Bhopal, including the emergency dump tank, Institute has a 30,000-gallon above-ground dump tank, which is twice the size of its 14,000-gallon above-ground MIC tanks. There is also a "dedicated sump system . . . where the MIC can be safely contained," with a capacity of 42,000 gallons − 140 percent the size of each of the 30,000-gallon underground MIC storage tanks at Institute, giving that plant an extra margin of safety in case of an accident.[73]

Instrument and control devices are also more extensive at Institute, and the plant there also has a computer system that increases plant safety. Union Carbide has tried to blur this crucial difference between the plants, stating, "The computer at Institute is for the plant production operations and to log in data and it does not operate safety equipment."[74] While it may not operate safety equipment directly, the computer system does log such things as pressures, temperatures, and chemical levels, which certainly impacts on safety, as it would give operators a clear record of what is going on in the plant − something glaringly absent on the night of December 2 in Bhopal.[75]

OSHA also notes that for MIC production at Institute, a "program has been developed to monitor the system through computerized reliable maintenance and visual observations . . . the reliable maintenance program is designed to determine and evaluate replacement frequency for valves, tank walls, instrumentation, and piping."[76]

Of course, in reading EPA and OSHA reports it isn't easy to distinguish between hyperbole and truth, since much is aimed at reassuring understandably nervous U.S. citizens that they needn't worry about poison gas inundating their communities. And indeed, after accidents like the August 11 release at Institute, the credibility of the EPA, OSHA, and the chemical industry further declined. Nonetheless, the differences between Bhopal and Institute are striking.

The contrast between the Bhopal plant and a number of other chemical plants in the industrialized world is even more glaring. *Newsweek* reports that in some plants in the U.S. and Europe, there is not only a computerized early warning system in operation, but a computer which "senses leaks when they occur, monitors their rate, concentration and toxicity, evaluates weather conditions and displays the anticipated cloud on a computer screen with the degree of danger for anything in its path." This system is linked with the phone system, and can alert the public by dialing phone numbers and playing recorded messages.[77]

At the Bayer plants in Antwerp, Belgium and Dormagen, West Germany, MIC is manufactured and directly processed into pesticides with very little storage. Storage tanks are equipped with extensive temperature and pressure gauges which regulate tank conditions and are hooked into an alarm system. Safety systems are designed not only for simple leaks, but also to handle major accidents. In one West German plant there is a full-time fire brigade, equipped with 50-foot-high mobile towers from which they can pour tremendous quantities of water onto any MIC leak, and a mobile chemical unit which can smother a leaking tank with foam in eight minutes and then suck up the gas at the rate of 46,000 gallons an hour.*[78]

Compare all this with Bhopal, where workers had to detect leaking gases with their eyes and noses; where the water spray system couldn't even reach the exploding gases; where the only computer on the premises was for the plant payroll and accounts payable; and where the only controls on key safety systems were manual, requiring workers to operate them in the middle of

---

*It should be noted, of course, that not all chemical plants in the industrialized countries have such equipment, and that the large majority of them remain unsafe. The point is that the situation in the Third World is even worse.

clouds of poison gas on the morning of December 3.

But leaving aside for a moment the question of the adequacy of the technology at the Bhopal plant, what of the more general argument that technology introduced into the Third World is of great benefit to these countries, and provides an important basis for economic self-sufficiency and independence? This will be discussed in more detail later, but here a few points need to be made. Certainly foreign capital introduces advanced technology into the underdeveloped countries, but what is crucial is that it is introduced on the basis of certain relations and conditions – most importantly the continuing economic and political domination of the underdeveloped countries by the developed ones. This determines how and for what purposes the technology is used, and who actually benefits.

For instance, it is ironic and also quite revealing to hear complaints about the technological backwardness of Third World countries when the industrialized countries of the West work so vigorously to preserve their relative monopoly of advanced technology. Decisions about where to locate factories, which processes to employ in various countries, and what technology to export – in short, what technology to transfer to whom – are all made with an eye to preserving both a competitive technological edge and the dominant economic and political position of the West as a whole over Third World countries, as well as preventing advanced technology from falling into the hands of the Soviet bloc.*

This generally means that advanced processes are concentrated in the industrialized countries, while labor-intensive work is done abroad. The U.S. electronics industry, which keeps research and development at home, while shipping assembly work to Asia, is a prime example. And, generally, whatever technology is shipped overseas is not really transferred to the host country – it remains the carefully protected property and knowledge of the "donor." The head of a government-sponsored

---

*And while the Soviet Union is neither as advanced technologically as the West, nor does it operate internationally in quite the same way, it too seeks to use its technology to advance its own global imperialist interests. Soviet trade- and technology-sharing agreements with India, especially in the state sector, are a case in point. (See chapter 6 for more on this.)

unit of New Delhi University in charge of Corporate Studies told the *New York Times*, "We are finding that the technology often just gets transferred to the premises of the subsidiary, not into the society as a whole. It stays within the walls of the factory."[79]

Union Carbide itself offers a good example of this. Warren Anderson claims that his corporation has behaved in an "exemplary fashion" in regard to transferring technology and technological know-how to the Third World. "We Mexicanized Mexico and Brazilianized Brazil and Indianized India and brought the people along, trained them, developed them, and there were no Americans in India."[80] Such talk is reminiscent of Richard Nixon's efforts to "Vietnamize" the Vietnam war – that is, to let others fight and die for U.S. interests. Similarly, Union Carbide's "Indianization" had little to do with putting an end to India's dependence and neocolonial control.

The plant in Bhopal is a case in point. This plant was expanded from a formulation unit to a production plant ostensibly to promote Indian self-reliance. But first of all, due in large part to the relatively backward state of the Indian economy, the technology utilized at the Bhopal plant was entirely imported from the U.S. parent. Union Carbide of India paid Union Carbide Corporation for engineering expenses and paid a "technical service fee" for use of UCC's technology, patents, and trademarks. Also, Indian personnel were trained to operate the Bhopal plant. But none of this made UCIL an independent agent. It remained dependent upon UCC to provide the information necessary to utilize the transferred technology. For instance, UCIL paid Union Carbide for "continuous know-how and safety audits";[81] it received operating licenses from the Indian government only on the basis that it would receive updated technological information from UCC; and there are reports that the Bhopal plant was in frequent communication with Institute on technical and production matters.[82]

Union Carbide also continued to control the technology it transferred through its overall ownership and control of UCIL. Nor did any of this technology become India's in any way; it remained the closely guarded proprietary knowledge of the corporation. Union Carbide's transfer of technology to Bhopal proved to be more a case of "skinning the ox twice," first charging

Union Carbide of India for the technology, then still maintaining control of it through the Bhopal facility's continued dependence upon UCC for technological assistance.[83]

A similar pattern prevails at the UCIL research and development laboratory in Bhopal. UCIL management has claimed that this facility, staffed entirely by Indians, is one of the most advanced in India, and because of it new pesticides could be discovered outside of the highly industrialized countries for the first time. But this laboratory doesn't operate independently of its U.S. parent. Its own director points out that it remains closely linked to UCC research facilities in the U.S., whose much larger data base is crucial for the R&D lab's functioning. And even if this facility did independently discover a new pesticide molecule, it would remain the property of UCC through its control of UCIL. Decisions on sharing or utilizing the new discovery would be made by UCC, in accordance with its interests, not the imperatives of Indian self-reliance, technological development, or increased agricultural production.

Education patterns in a country like India afford another example of how foreign capital creates and perpetuates technological backwardness, while strengthening its own position. For example, India has the fifth largest number of technical graduates of any country in the world, but relative to the country's huge population and needs, this number is woefully inadequate. In terms of scientific personnel per thousand population, India ranked third from the bottom, above only Ghana and Kenya, among the 24 nations covered by a UNESCO study.

Moreover, many of these highly educated and skilled people end up working not for indigenous industries but for multinationals, or emigrating abroad where wages and the general standard of living are higher. It is often said, for example, that the British medical system would fall apart were it not for Indian (and Pakistani) doctors. Yet the 70 percent of the Indian people who live in the rural areas rarely if ever see a doctor.

In fact, the whole Indian educational system is lopsidedly skewed to meet the needs of industry – including foreign industry – even though the development of agriculture is vitally important to the advance of the entire Indian economy and to improving the lives of the Indian people. But as of 1975, India produced twenty-five times more graduates — 107,900 vs. 4,000 — with degrees in science and engineering than in agricultural studies.[84]

In sum, neither in terms of the overall situation in India, nor in terms of the particular situation in Bhopal, can it be said that the main problem is the existence of "too much" complex, state-of-the-art technology which the people simply can't handle. In fact, as we have seen, a major reason for the massacre in Bhopal was not too much, but way too little technology in the plant's basic design; and the effort of Union Carbide and its apologists to blame it on "Indian backwardness" is blatantly false and an obvious attempt to conceal the corporation's own responsibility.

3 | Procedures, Projections, and Danger in the Slums

It is true that a host of procedural violations – overfilling the MIC tanks, shutting down the refrigeration unit, turning off safety equipment, etc. – contributed to the December 2-3 disaster. The question is: why did these violations occur?

In the early 1970s, when plans were made to expand the Bhopal plant from a formulation unit to an integrated production operation, the future looked bright for pesticides. Between 1972 and 1983, global pesticide sales increased from $8.1 billion to $12.8 billion a year. Due in large part to a number of U.S.-sponsored agricultural programs like the "Green Revolution" in India, the amount of pesticides consumed by "low and middle income" countries rose from 8 percent to 15 percent of world production. Pesticide use nearly tripled between 1966-67 and 1970-71, and soon India had the tenth largest pesticide market in the world, and seemingly one of the most promising for the future.[1]

But these optimistic projections never came to pass. The unit at the Bhopal plant which produced alpha napthol was plagued with technical problems. More importantly, the great hopes for the "Green Revolution" were never fully realized, as agricultural production in India was confronted by deep contradictions.

The rate of annual growth of agricultural production was

actually declining, from 3.3 percent a year between 1950–51 and 1965–66, to 2.7 percent a year between 1965–66 and 1983–84.[2] Farm income as a percent of the gross value of agricultural output declined from 49 percent in 1970–71 to 42 percent in 1980–81, and on average remained seriously low.[3] And drought struck India in 1977, exacerbating these long-term problems. After pesticide consumption tripled between 1966–67 and 1970–71, growth tapered off in the following years and between 1980 and 1983 pesticide use increased a total of only 15 percent.[4] Declining incomes forced many farmers to turn to cheaper pesticides than Carbide's, and the not-so-rapidly expanding market meant Carbide faced increasing competition from other types of pesticides, organophosphates and new synthetic pyrethriods. "The market never exceeded half our capacity," UCIL's managing director, V.P. Gokhale, said. "If the market would have expanded, we would have had a gold mine."[5]

The Bhopal plant had a 5,000-ton production capacity, but in 1982 only 2,308 tons of pesticides were produced. Output dropped to 1,647 tons in 1983 and to 1,000 in 1984.[6] Instead of the $6 million annual profit projected eight years earlier,[7] the plant lost nearly $4 million in 1984.[8] At the same time, UCIL as a whole faced a variety of economic problems. On UCIL's 50th anniversary, in July 1984, *Fortune India* wrote, "The company has apparently run out of steam. Sales are almost stagnant, profitability declining."[9] During the same period, the parent sales were also flat, and profits declined from $890 million in 1980 to $79 million in 1983.[10]

UCC's response, from 1983 on, was to try to wholesale chemicals produced in Bhopal to other producers, sell parts of the plant, and cut costs with a vengeance.[11] UCIL forced the plant's two unions to accept a contract cutting back staffing in the name of improving "average productivity" and "eliminating such work practices which are not conducive to efficient working of the plant."[12] In the two years before the accident, total permanent employment was cut from 850 to 642. In the MIC unit, staffing was cut from eleven operators and one supervisor per shift to five operators and one supervisor. The field maintenance staff was cut from four per shift to two, and the crew in the maintenance shop from six to four. Between one-half and two-thirds of the skilled engineers, familiar with the MIC unit, also left the factory as its fortunes declined.[13] The International Federation of Chemical, Energy and General Workers' Unions reports that workers were forced into early retirement, and 300 temporary workers were laid off. One hundred fifty permanent workers who were laid off were pooled and assigned to jobs as needed. "The workers. . . said that employees were often assigned to jobs they were not qualified to do. . . . If the workers refused to do the job which they were assigned on grounds they were not trained, their salaries were reduced."[14]

Educational requirements and training levels were also reduced. According to *India Today,* "In 1977–78, when work on the MIC plant started, only first class B.Sc. graduates or those with a diploma in engineering were taken as operators. They were subject to 6 months theoretical training and then trained on the job. That is no longer true, and there are cases of operators without an academic science background and, what is more, they no longer have to undergo the same rigorous training as before."[15] Also, people were transferred from other plants who didn't know the system. For example, the head of the agricultural products division, which oversaw operations in Bhopal, had recently been transferred from the battery division.

There also were cuts in routine maintenance. As the new agreement between the company and unions put it, maintenance previously done on all shifts would now be "carried out on the General shift as far as possible."[16] Praful Bidwai reports, "Maintenance engineers began to complain of shortages of critical components. . . instrument technicians had to do with incompatible gauges and to replace old ones with new sets of defective indicators. . . leaking valves were allowed to leak unless the magnitude of the discharge increased to unbearable levels. . . preventive anti-corrosion maintenance. . . has suffered a steep decline in quality. Equipment checks and testing of samples of materials also appear to have become less and less frequent since 1982."[17]

The results of these staffing and maintenance cuts were all too apparent on the night of December 2. The swing shift supervisor, who was on duty the night of the disaster and ordered the water washing of the pipelines without insisting on inserting a slip blind, was new to the plant. The worker performing the job was also new and had little training. Maintenance supervisors (rather than the shift supervisor) were generally responsible for making sure slip blinds were inserted; but the maintenance supervisors were eliminated from the second and third shifts two weeks before the disaster.*[18]

The clogged bleeder valves, leaky valves, and the jumper line, which together led to the entry of water into tank 610, were also the result of reduced maintenance and cost-cutting efforts. Keeping MIC cool, through refrigeration, is an important safety precaution because it makes the chemical much less reactive. Union Carbide's publication, "Methyl Isocyanate," states that refrigeration will "not eliminate the possibility of a violent reaction, if contamination occurs. It will, however, increase the time available for detection . . . and safe disposal of the material before the reaction rate reaches a dangerous speed."[20] The summer before the accident, the MIC tank refrigeration unit was shut down to save electricity and the freon coolant was removed for use in another part of the plant. In addition, the company cut operating costs by routinely shutting down the plant's key safety systems — the flare tower and the vent gas scrubber — when the MIC production unit was not operating, even though MIC was being stored in the tanks.[21]

Standard operating procedures were increasingly ignored and dangerous shortcuts became the rule of the day. *Now* magazine reports managers used to tell workers that if the standard procedures were followed, the plant couldn't run.[22] All this, of course, was the result of Union Carbide Corporation's decision to cut back because of economic difficulties. It is therefore rather stunning to read in the *New York Times* that "If preventative maintenance is a new concept, it should be more thoroughly taught," and that "The idea of spending money now to save money later is a concept completely alien" — to India![23]

---

*The night shift supervisor's decision to wait until after tea time before investigating the reported MIC leak appears incredibly negligent. But it was probably a normal reaction to frequent, minor releases of MIC. Union Carbide's 1982 inspection report noted that leaking valves were "fairly common," and Bhopal's operating manual even states, "A certain amount of toxic gas release is unavoidable and unpredictable."[19]

A History of Danger

The whole safety history of the Bhopal plant further argues that responsibility for the disaster rests with Union Carbide Corporation. For even before the severe cutbacks, the factory had a record of dangerous operations, disregard for any except the most petty safety measures, a number of serious accidents, including one death, and complaints by workers that the plant was unsafe.

In addition to the host of deadly chemicals used at the plant, its end products, Sevin and Temik, are listed as "moderately" and "extremely" hazardous, respectively, by the World Health Organization. Temik is the pesticide responsible for the poisoning of California watermelons in the summer of 1985. While Union Carbide states that its carbamate pesticides are safe because they are biodegradable and don't persist in the environment, Temik has reportedly poisoned groundwater in the U.S. alone in Wisconsin, Maine, Virginia, North Carolina, Florida, and New York.[24]

Both Dr. L. D. Loya, the plant's chief medical officer, and U. Nanda, the factory safety director, claimed that the workers were warned about all the chemicals during "job safety analysis."[25] According to H. M. Zariwala, head of the Union Carbide Workmen's Union at the Bhopal plant, "The safety manual was sent from West Virginia but it was kept by management and no worker had seen it."[26] The operations manual wasn't even translated into Hindi – despite the fact that the majority of the workers did not speak English – and if workers wrote in the log books in Hindi they were reprimanded.[27]

Workers insisted they had come to understand the toxicity of the chemicals they worked with not through the manual or "job safety analysis," but a different way – through bitter experience. "We learned they were dangerous because of their effects," said one worker, who told of many workers suffering from contact with Temik. Zariwala agreed: "The management never told the workers about the dangers of MIC – we came to know it only by experience. Workers used to vomit, feel uneasy, or get pains in their chests, so we knew it was dangerous."

Protection for employees working with these chemicals was virtually nonexistent. The mask given Temik workers was a three-by-four-inch patch of cotton. These masks and the gloves workers were given didn't prevent them from frequent skin contact with Temik, which they then just washed off. Often workers didn't even wear these simple protective devices because the plant, which wasn't air conditioned, was too hot. Workers also said that general weakness often resulted from long-term exposure to the chemicals and that one worker died in January 1984 from such exposure.

Between 1978 and 1984, there were six major accidents at the plant which were precursors of the December 2–3 disaster in a number of respects, resulting in the death of one worker and the exposure of some fifty workers and hundreds of nearby residents to toxic gases. For example, in November 1978, there was a major fire in the naptha storage area, sending clouds of smoke billowing over the neighboring areas and doing roughly one-half million dollars worth of property damage. In December 1981, phosgene spilled on a worker as he was opening the flanges of a pipeline to do maintenance work. He died the next day. In February 1982, twenty-five workers were overcome and taken to the hospital when a pump seal was damaged and phosgene leaked. In October 1982, a combination of chloroform, MIC and hydrochloric acid leaked from a loose-fitting valve in the MIC production unit. Three workers suffered severe burns, fifteen others were treated for less severe exposure, and many people in the community fled after experiencing the tearing and choking effects of MIC.[28]

While company experts did little about these warning signs, plant workers – whose lack of "safety mentality" and "mechanical sense" we have heard so much about – were quite alarmed over the dangerous conditions in the plant and had been raising safety issues since 1974. For example, in 1982, after the death of the one worker from phosgene poisoning, the Workmen's Union printed up 6,000 posters and put them up around the factory and throughout Bhopal. "Beware, Beware, Beware – Accidents, Accidents, Accidents," the headline read. "Thousands of workers and lakhs* of citizens of Bhopal are being affected by the poisonous gas and their life is in peril." The posters warned of the many accidents in the plant, the labor laws

*One lakh equals one hundred thousand.

being violated, and the inadequacy of plant safety measures.

Union Carbide's response to the campaign was to harass the workers involved. Workers were not allowed to have meetings in the plant on trade union or political issues, so a series of plant gate rallies and meetings, on safety among other things, was held. Three union activists were fired, ostensibly for unrelated causes, but workers and residents of Bhopal are convinced otherwise.

If Union Carbide's safety practices were terrible inside the plant, they were nonexistent outside. Carbide was, of course, well aware of the deadliness and volatility of MIC and the host of other poisons used at the plant, as their various publications make clear. But Carbide didn't bother to inform the community of these potential dangers, conduct emergency training, or organize evacuation plans. Instead, it raised no objections as new shanty settlements sprung up near its gates, and insisted the plant was safe right up through the night of the disaster.

People in the surrounding communities knew, by and large, that pesticides were being produced, and a few had experienced some of the noxious effects from the gases produced inside the plant. But no one, in the words of one resident of thirteen years, "had any idea that such a deadly poison was being used." Even Bhopal's medical community was kept largely in the dark.

The concluding article in the *New York Times* series on Bhopal alludes to the fact that people living near the Carbide factory didn't understand its potential danger, and sums up that, "Public education is critical in developing countries, where people often do not understand the hazards of toxic substances. Repeated drills and clear warning signals are needed."[29] But who was responsible for this lack of understanding and the absence of warnings and drills? The *Times* implies that the problem was Third World ignorance. But the problem in Bhopal was that Carbide systematically hid the danger from the community!

Managing director Gokhale refused to answer any questions about why Carbide hadn't informed the people of Bhopal of the dangers of MIC.[30] But Dr. Loya, the plant's chief medical officer, admitted that Carbide had never told the community about the danger, save for a few in Bhopal's medical community. Why? "You see in our country, if I say that 'I'm carrying a deadly thing in my pocket,' people just turn you out of the town. [They] don't allow you to remain there, even though you aren't going to use it.... Here people are so emotional... if you tell them that, then the next day there will be a big procession and do-to-do and la-de-da, 'will you please stop this factory, we don't want it,' even though it is not dangerous. Telling the truth is sometimes a difficult problem in our country."

But the truth, and some elementary training, could have saved hundreds of lives and alleviated the suffering of tens of thousands. An Indian Council of Medical Research (ICMR) report, written nine days after the disaster, notes that "It is general knowledge that those that stayed indoors and closed their doors and windows were less affected. So also those that covered their faces with wet cloth."[31] But these simple precautions were unknown to the people living next to the factory.

Union Carbide's policy of hiding the hazards of its plant played itself out in devastating fashion on the night of December 2–3, significantly augmenting the death and injury toll. The gas exploded into the atmosphere around 12:30 a.m., but by most accounts no alarm was sounded to warn the surrounding community until one and one-half to two hours later. This was due to Union Carbide's policy of not sounding the plant's loud public alarm out of concern that it would arouse public fears and opposition to the plant.

Even Union Carbide in its March 20 report claimed that the alarm had not been sounded until 1:00. According to its own reconstruction of the accident, this was a full forty minutes *after* employees realized that a massive leak was underway. Yet Carbide's report makes little of it. It's as if nothing abnormal happened.[32]

A number of Indian publications have reported that the alarm was turned on briefly at 1:00 a.m., quickly turned off, and only turned on again sometime after 2:00 a.m. This sequence of events would explain why there were some reports that an alarm sounded around 1:00, while most put it after 2:00. According to *Business India*, two different types of alarms were turned on together around 1:00 on December 3 – "a loud public siren which warns the public in the surrounding areas and a muted siren within the factory.... In accordance with procedures introduced in 1982–83, five minutes later the [outside] sirens were first switched off and only the muted siren was switched on. This procedural modification was apparently made so that the people living around the factory do not panic!....On the night of 2–3 December, the loud public siren was restarted only around 2:30 a.m."*[33]

Nor did Union Carbide in any way help to evacuate people once the disaster occurred. Carbide workers quickly realized what had happened, and most, alerted to the wind direction by a wind sock that hung over the MIC production plant, ran in the opposite direction to safety, as they had previously been instructed to do by management. And given the plant's defective safety systems, there was little – if anything – they could have done to stop the gas leak if they had stayed. (No Carbide workers on duty that night died from exposure to MIC.) But there was no wind sock outside the plant. The company had four buses, ostensibly for evacuating the neighboring population (or rather a tiny percentage of it), but in the early morning hours of December 3 they stood idle. Carbide never did inform authorities in Bhopal of the accident because, according to the *New York Times*, "management had an informal policy of not involving the local authorities in gas leaks."[34]

Throughout the night, even as people were dying in their thousands, local Carbide officials compounded Bhopal's medical crisis by hewing to the line that MIC wasn't a deadly poison, and saying nothing about the possibility of it producing toxic reaction products. Doctors at Hamidia Hospital reported calling Dr. Loya shortly after 1:00 a.m. and being told that MIC "is *not* poisonous."[35] Dr. Loya later claimed he told the doctors that MIC "can cause pulmonary edema" (filling of the lungs with fluids). When asked if he told them it could be fatal, he said, "Frankly speaking, I told them that acute pulmonary edema can cause death," an odd and superfluous addendum when talking to doctors. Dr. Ranjid Singh, the commissioner of the Bhopal administrative division, stated that works manager Mukund told

---

*Had the public siren sounded earlier, at least many would have been awakened before the toxic gases were upon them. But they may not have understood the significance of the siren. As part of its policy of keeping people in the dark, Carbide had never informed neighboring residents of the meaning of the plant's alarms.

him that MIC "causes great irritation in the eyes. . . I asked him what happens if you inhale too much. . . could people die? He said such a thing has never happened." It was happening even as he spoke.*[36]

"But We Didn't Know"

Union Carbide has argued that corporate headquarters simply didn't know about all the violations of company procedures and safety standards. If it had, these conditions would never have been tolerated; in fact, the plant wouldn't even have been allowed to operate.[43] Of course, this contention immediately undermines some of Union Carbide's other claims. The corporation has argued that it takes "great steps to insure that the plants of our affiliates. . . are properly equipped with safeguards and that employees are properly trained,"[44] and then claimed that it didn't know what was going on in Bhopal. It has also called safety a "top priority" for the corporation, but then called it a "local" matter –

---

*A similar pattern of delayed warnings and downplaying of medical hazards was evident during and immediately after the August 11, 1985 leak at Carbide's Institute plant. Company officials first admitted to waiting until twenty minutes after the leak before notifying emergency officials, which they later changed to eleven minutes because the earlier figure, they claimed, was based on wrong information on the automatic telephone log. They then waited another sixteen minutes before sounding the public warning siren.[37]

Company officials also first announced that aldicarb oxime was the principal component involved in the leak. The company doctor, Bipin Avashia, said aldicarb oxime is a very minor irritant that would have no long-term effects.[38] A chemical industry spokesperson, interviewed on ABC's *Nightline* program, said the chemical was less harmful than aspirin.[39] But according to Union Carbide's own internal memos – sent directly to Dr. Avashia – aldicarb oxime is as lethal and dangerous as MIC.[40] The company then subsequently announced that aldicarb oxime had only made up less than 1 percent of the toxic chemicals released in the leak. The largest component, they now said, was the solvent, methylene chloride.[41] This chemical has been shown to cause eye irritation, respiratory problems, and lung and liver damage in humans. A study by the National Toxicology Program says that methylene chloride has caused cancer in some laboratory animals. But Carbide officials say that neither methylene chloride, aldicarb oxime, nor any of the other chemicals that leaked are life threatening or would have any lasting health effects.[42]

unlike key financial decisions that are handled at the top.[45]

More fundamentally, given the relationship between UCC and UCIL, in particular the parent's overall control and subsidiary's all-round dependence upon the parent, it would seem that Union Carbide headquarters would have had to know what was going on at the Bhopal plant. And all the available evidence points exactly to that.

Union Carbide operates a far-flung operation through some 95 divisions, departments, subsidiaries, and affiliates with over 600 facilities in countries on every continent. The center of this global web is Union Carbide Corporation's headquarters in Danbury. The various outposts of Carbide's industrial empire report back either directly or through other Carbide subsidiaries to Danbury. In the case of UCIL, UCC's chain of command stretches from Danbury to the company's Union Carbide Eastern in Hong Kong, a 100 percent UCC-owned subsidiary whose chairman is also a corporate vice president of UCC. UC Eastern in turn has three directors on the UCIL board, one of whom is UCIL's vice-chairman, and oversees its operation. Danbury also has its own representative, an executive vice president of the corporation, on the UCIL board of directors.[46]

Danbury has overall financial control of all its subsidiaries, and makes key investment and strategic decisions in light of its global interests. This financial decision-making power gave it knowledge and fundamental control of the Bhopal plant. Union Carbide Corporation approved the $20 million expenditure to set up pesticide production in Bhopal. In fact, any capital expenditure by UCIL over $500,000 has to be approved by UCC, as does any change in a given capital expenditure, giving UCC control over major safety-related equipment expenses and the means to determine if budgeted equipment is not purchased.[47] Corporate headquarters also oversees UCIL's annual budget — which would certainly reflect things like the reduced manpower and curtailed maintenance that were at the root of the Bhopal plant's various procedural violations.[48]

Another central factor in Union Carbide Corporation's knowledge and control of its Indian and other subsidiaries is its control of key technology. The precise details of its organizational structure and the number of memos that passed between Bhopal and Danbury aside, UCC knew what was going on in Bhopal because without the technological guidance and updates, including questions of design, operating procedures, and safety practices that only it can provide, the Bhopal plant could not have functioned. This is why there have been numerous reports that Danbury knew plenty about the nuts and bolts of what was happening in Bhopal, including such details as the shutting down of the refrigeration unit and the construction of the jumper line between the RVVH and the PVH, even though headquarters has refused to comment on the details of its relationship with UCIL or produce any of the relevant communications.*[49]

Beyond this, Union Carbide's own safety audits — one of Bhopal and one of its Institute plant — demonstrate not only the company's involvement in matters of safety and the fact that it knew about many of the dangers existing at Bhopal well in advance of the December 2-3 disaster, but also an approach which almost totally ignored the danger of a major accident.

A Union Carbide Corporation Safety survey team audited the Bhopal plant in May 1982. This report, which was sent to Bombay (UCIL headquarters are in Bombay), Hong Kong, and Institute, W. Va., listed a total of 61 hazards, 30 of them considered major and 11 in the dangerous phosgene/MIC units, and warned of possible leaks that represent "either a higher potential for a serious incident or more serious consequences if an incident should occur." Many of the conditions listed were elements in the December 2–3 disaster. The report cites as areas of concern "procedures training and enforcement, together with attention to the equipment and mechanical deficiencies" and "deficiencies in safety valve and instrument maintenance programs." It notes that "filter cleaning operations are performed without slipblinding process line. Leaking valves could create serious exposures during this process."

The report warns that the "pressure gauge on the phosgene tank was bad, showing no pressure, even though the tank was in

*The Indian government has claimed it would be able to produce documents, seized when the Bhopal plant was taken over, showing that Union Carbide headquarters and the subsidiary were in constant communication about safety and other matters.[50]

service," and "frequent pressure gauge failure is a problem in all units." It states that "operator (and technical personnel, to a degree) turnover appears to pose a serious problem in the plant." And it also calls attention to the fact that "no water spray protection has been provided for fire protection or vapor cloud suppression" in the MIC or other storage areas.

Despite all this, the Bhopal plant is given a basically clean bill of health: "No situations involving imminent danger or requiring immediate correction were noted."* The company claims that all of these matters had been fixed before the disaster and hadn't contributed to it. As already shown, the evidence overwhelmingly contradicts this assertion. Poorly trained personnel, rapid turnover, leaking valves, shoddy gauges, and a water spray that couldn't reach high enough to douse the MIC roaring out of the plant were all elements in the disaster.[51]

Union Carbide's neglect of major safety dangers at the Bhopal plant is demonstrated in even starker fashion by a safety report in September 1984, just three months before the disaster. This internal Union Carbide report on the MIC plant at Institute classified two safety problems as "major concerns," one being the possibility of a "runaway reaction in the MIC unit storage tanks."† One might have thought that this report would have been forwarded to Bhopal, since it was Union Carbide's other MIC production facility. But Union Carbide never bothered to send it.[52]

When this report came to light, in the aftermath of the disaster, Union Carbide's safety chief tried to explain headquarters' actions by claiming that "there was no reason to share" the report because the two plants had different types of cooling systems.[53]

It is true that one of the sources of contamination which could trigger a runaway reaction in the Institute plant is leakage from the brine cooling system, and Bhopal's MIC tank refrigeration unit didn't use brine. But that was only *one* of the possible sources of contamination the report listed. The report stated that a

---

*Other major safety questions – the plant's location, the design of its safety devices, and community education – were also ignored.

†The other major concern was the potential for "serious chloroform overexposures" in the MIC unit.

"catastrophic failure of the tank" could arise from "a combination of situations and possibilities," and noted that there "have been instances of water contamination of the unit tanks in the past from several sources...."

Further, the report lists thirty-six separate items needing correction, including fourteen recommendations for "recovery/reaction" in the MIC unit and ten for the MIC storage unit. The report concludes, "This combination of water and catalyst contamination possibilities, reduced surveillance, increased residence time, and an experience-based low level of concern towards the potential hazard leads the team to conclude that a real potential for a serious incident exists." Every one of these last four major items figured prominently in the disaster at Bhopal.

After the catastrophe, Warren Anderson told the *Hartford Courant*, "'The question of a massive discharge just never occurred to anybody; therefore, it was never provided for.'"[54] The September 1984 report on Institute − along with all of Carbide's other publications warning of the toxicity and volatility of MIC − proves that this is nothing but a cavalier attempt to excuse the deaths of thousands. That Carbide never bothered to provide for a massive disaster simply reflects the fact that the corporation considered cutting costs of greater importance than Indian lives.

Living in the Shadows

The densely packed slums that sit in the very shadow of the Bhopal plant, constructed from scraps and refuse, stand in sharp contrast to Union Carbide's $20 million factory. These shanty colonies, and the rest of Bhopal, illustrate something of the typical pattern of imperialist-sponsored development in the Third World today, and particularly how foreign capital's introduction of advanced technology does not result in the growth of a well-developed and articulated economy and society as a whole.*
This pattern was central in turning the gas leak in Bhopal from a

---

*It should be emphasized here that, relative to the city of Bhopal overall, the Union Carbide plant was quite modern. On the other hand, relative to the technology required to provide for adequate safety or a worst-case situation, the "typical" industrial accident into a disaster of immense proportions.

Bhopal retains much of its pre-twentieth-century character, with the pulse and rhythms of a country town: cows and goats roam the streets, farmers sell their produce on dusty streets or open-air markets, and goods are often hauled by ox cart. Union Carbide's Bhopal facilities are part of the corporation's transportation, communications, and marketing network which crisscrosses the globe. But in old Bhopal, the historical heart of the city, communications are from a different era. The streets are narrow, often more like alleys that wind between buildings constructed hundreds of years ago, before motorized transport. Most people get around on foot, bicycle, or sometimes by bus. Very few people have cars or even motor scooters.

The marketing network of Bhopal is mainly a large number of tiny shops – often ten feet wide or less – that line the streets, usually selling a narrow range of products. In some, one finds high tech imports – TVs, radios, or cameras; the one next door may be selling handicrafts; outside a street vendor could be selling just bananas or grapes. Less than one in a hundred has a telephone in Bhopal. (In the state of Madhya Pradesh as a whole, phones are even more rare; there is one phone for every 670 people.)[55]

A plentiful water supply was one reason Carbide located in Bhopal, and it has never run short. Yet many people in Bhopal don't have piped water, and Lake Bhopal remains stagnant and polluted. Carbide uses thousands of kilowatts of electricity daily, but many homes in Bhopal have none, and barely 50 percent of the villages in Madhya Pradesh are electrified. Carbide boasts of its large staff of scientists; in Madhya Pradesh 72 percent of the population – and 84 percent of the women – are illiterate. The factory claims to have an up-to-date medical clinic; in Bhopal, which has more extensive medical facilities than any other city in the state, there is about one doctor for every 800 people; in Madhya Pradesh as a whole, there is one for every 11,600 people.

---

plant was not nearly modern enough. This contradiction itself is a sharp expression of the quality and amount of technology that is introduced into Third World countries, and who actually controls it.

In the U.S. there is a doctor for every 460 people.[56]

Ganesh War is a hotel worker who lives with his wife and infant child in J.P. Nagar, the shanty colony directly across the street from the factory and no more than 100 yards from the tower from which the gases exploded on December 3. Their eight-by-ten-foot makeshift hut is like most in the colony, made of bits gathered by hook or by crook. A variety of wooden poles, branches, and bamboo make up the frame of the shelter. The walls are an assortment of plastic tarps, scrap wood, and burlap; the roof is a combination of straw mats, bamboo, and tin; the floor is dirt and a few paving stones. Shafts of light stream in through the dozens of cracks and holes in the collage of material that makes up the outer shell of Ganesh's home. The family's furniture consists of a single wood frame bed, a small sewing table, and a chair. Their belongings are piled in one corner in burlap bags and a five-gallon tin container.

Conditions at J.P. Nagar are extremely cramped. Ganesh's home shares a wall with another hut and is separated from others by alleys as narrow as three or four feet. All told, the colony is something less than a quarter mile long and fifty-plus yards deep. Yet there are 500 households and 3,000 people crammed together in single-story dwellings here. The situation in other shanties is similar. Bhopal's 1975 town plan lists Kazi Camp as having 580 households and 3,160 people on an area of 6.3 hectares – a density of 527 people per hectare (2.47 acres). Other shanty settlements in Bhopal have population densities as high as 925 per hectare, again in single-story dwellings.[57]

The density isn't accidental. People have set up their homes with literally nothing, cramming into whatever vacant land can be found in the city, near possible employment. Homes spring up around water and electric lines that can be tapped into. One state government official explained, "Most of our slums are long and narrow strips along roadsides; this way people can take advantage of the infrastructure existing there." Ganesh's hut, like most, is lit by a single bulb hanging from the ceiling. The people of J.P. Nagar had managed to hook into a nearby power line. There is no running water or sewage system here, only several common wells for water and roadside drainage ditches or stagnant pools for its disposal. In one area, for a bit of privacy, four burlap sheets have been hung up around a dirt depression that serves as a community toilet. Shanty dwellers are lucky compared to many migrant workers in Bhopal who have no homes at all. They are forced to camp out near their jobs – something that one sees throughout India, near construction sites in particular – or sleep on the streets or at the railway station. One official said that at any given time there are 60,000 of these migrant laborers in Bhopal.

At a December 6, 1984 press conference, amid a furor over the fact that Union Carbide's Bhopal plant was located in a highly populated area, Union Carbide explained that "The plant's location, three to four miles from the center of Bhopal, was selected by Union Carbide India Limited more than 17 years ago. At that time, the area was not densely populated." But "land is scarce and the population often gravitates towards areas that contain manufacturing facilities. That's how so many people came to be living near the fences surrounding our property."[58]

But Carbide's claim that its plant was originally located "three or four miles" from the center of Bhopal and well outside populated areas is simply a sleight-of-hand. Initially, in 1969, the factory was formally outside city limits and many shanty colonies existing in 1984 had not yet been established. But even then it was close to areas that had been inhabited for many years. Union Carbide President Alec Flamm told *Chemical Week* magazine that slides of the plant in 1969 showed "grass and water buffalo, nothing else in sight."[59] The photographer must have had his back to the city.

The factory is located on the northern edge of Bhopal, roughly two miles from the heart of the old city, where the upper and lower parts of Lake Bhopal meet. This area has been inhabited since 1010 A.D., some years before Carbide arrived, and is one of the most densely populated in the city. The railway station, an important population center for fifty years, is roughly a mile from the plant. The bus station is a half mile or so away. Hamidia and Sultania hospitals, the telephone exchange, the Jama Masjid (one of the largest mosques in Asia), the General Post Office, and numerous banks, shops, schools, residences, and hotels are located here. All were enveloped in gas on the morning of December 3. Thus even if none of the newer shanty settlements closest to the plant had existed, tens of thousands would still have inhaled the killer gases.[60]

Though some of the shanty colonies that were adjacent to the plant in 1984 didn't exist in 1969 when the plant opened as a formulation unit, many *did* exist years before the MIC production unit began operation in 1980. Bhopal's town plan was published in 1975, the year Union Carbide received its license to manufacture MIC-based pesticides and about two years before construction on the MIC unit began. The plan notes the existence of a number of slums adjacent to or near Carbide, such as Kazi Camp, Chhola, and Chandbad, with a population of around 5,000. But these nearby settlements neither slowed down Carbide's expansion plans nor caused it to consider relocating the plant.[61]

The fact that Union Carbide was right in the midst of a well-populated area wasn't accidental, but rather had everything to do with the dynamics of its operations. Carbide was situated in Bhopal because the city is strategically located in the center of India, at the hub of rail lines and roadways linking India's major cities — Bombay, Delhi and Calcutta — as well as the main wheat-growing areas in the north and the rice-producing lands in the south and east. The Madhya Pradesh government offered Carbide cheap and guaranteed supplies of power and water as inducements for locating in Bhopal.[62] And the land itself that Carbide was located on was leased to them at rock bottom rates — "any cheaper and we would have been giving them a subsidy," said one former official.

Carbide also wanted to be near the amenities of a city like Bhopal to attract and keep the scientists and engineers essential to the plant's operation. Finally, cheap labor is one of India's prime attractions for foreign capital — and pools of wage labor are concentrated in the cities. UCIL paid its regular blue-collar employees at the Bhopal plant an average of 1,200 rupees a month, or about $92 — $3.75 a day.* As if these wages were too exorbitant, the company also hired some seventy contract laborers to do a variety of jobs including offloading, canteen work and security for ten to twelve rupees — less than $1 a day.[63] Prox-

---

*It is an interesting commentary in its own right that, in India, this represents fairly high pay.

imity to its labor pool was no doubt a consideration in Carbide's choice of location. Most of its workers were far too poor to own any kind of transportation; the only way they could get to work was on foot.

Union Carbide claims that these wretched shanties sprang up around its Bhopal plant as people came in search of work – in effect making the company the unwitting and unwilling victim of the benefits it provided the community. But even on this level, the benefits that Union Carbide bestowed on the local economy weren't nearly as great as the corporation and U.S. press reports lead one to believe. With slightly over 800 employees in a city of 800,000 – which also has fifteen other large or medium-sized factories – the Carbide plant was definitely not the main source of livelihood in Bhopal, although it did offer generally higher wages.[64] Certainly some living in the slums surrounding it worked at the plant, had relatives who did, or were employed in businesses dependent on the Bhopal factory for their existence. But even in the neighboring slums, Carbide wasn't the main employer. Most living there are casual laborers, hauling goods by hand truck, carrying bundles of cotton or agricultural produce, or digging trenches or carrying cement at construction sites. Most others are engaged in a variety of petty occupations such as rolling and selling the small "bidi" cigarettes, working in small repair shops, peddling goods, or working in offices or other factories. The greatest benefit many shanty dwellers got from the Carbide factory was the chance to tap clandestinely into the electricity lines leading to it, or to use refuse from the plant to construct their homes.

Thus, while some people worked at the Bhopal plant or in other ways were dependent on it, there are also larger factors that help to explain the rise of slums such as these. The "Green Revolution" in India – of which the Bhopal plant was a part – is an example. Designed in the 1960s under the auspices of the Ford Foundation, this "revolution" was predicated upon the application of modern technology to agriculture. Its defenders claimed it would bring agricultural abundance and self-sufficiency to India. Instead, it brought the increasing concentration of the means of agricultural production in the hands of the well-to-do, and also led to the increasing lack of investment in traditional or dry farming, the forcible removal of peasants from their land to make way for modern forms of production, and the continuing impoverishment of the countryside. These results have combined to drive millions off the land and into sprawling urban slums, in search of whatever bit of work can be found. Slum dwellers in Bhopal talked of people in their home villages having so little land that they are unable to feed their own children off of it, and so few jobs that even five rupees a day was double what they made in the villages.

It is precisely developments like these, not mentioned by Union Carbide or the U.S. press but integral to the post–World War 2 operation of imperialism, that have made burgeoning shantytowns constructed in the shadow of modern industry – and industrial disasters that take the lives of thousands of these shanty dwellers – a global phenomenon.[65] On November 19, 1984, just two weeks before the disaster in Bhopal, propane exploded at a Pemex factory in San Juan Ixhuatepec, near Mexico City; over 450 of the people living around the plant were killed. In February 1984, a leaking gas line caught fire in Cubatao, an industrial center in southern Brazil; its victims were again scores of people living in makeshift settlements a stone's throw from dangerous industrial facilities.

4 | The Gas Chamber

There are nights when Nafisubi Ali's four-year-old son wakes up screaming and starts running outside; he is still haunted by nightmares of the gassing of Bhopal. But the town's night of horror doesn't live on only in dreams. Nafisubi's family and tens of thousands like hers still suffer from a host of crippling after-effects.

An April 1985 report says that on average, two gas-affected residents of Bhopal die each day.[1] In July 1985 — seven months after the disaster — an estimated 50,000 to 60,000 were still severely debilitated. Doctors can only guess what the long-term effects, including carcinogenic, mutagenic (effect on chromosomes, leading to genetic mutations), and teratogenic (effect on human embryos), might be. To people like Nafisubi and her family, it is clear that the nightmare is far from over. "The doctors who say we are getting better are lying," she declares.

Union Carbide Corporation immediately expressed its concern for the victims and stated it was "in constant contact with appropriate governmental representatives in offering and giving whatever aid we can provide to the people suffering from this unprecedented accident."[2] Warren Anderson, a group of company representatives, and several U.S. doctors left for India on

December 4, with the stated aim of facilitating the relief effort. The Indian government also declared its first priority was caring for the victims.

But for thousands the medical care has been a prolongation of the horror of the gassing. In fact, the magnitude of the catastrophe has been greatly compounded by the medical intrigue in its aftermath, which many people in Bhopal have paid or will pay for with their lives, or with a lifetime of suffering.

Union Carbide had unleashed a chemical horror upon Bhopal that no medical system in the world, particularly in the Third World, could have dealt with. With limited facilities, thousands of patients streaming into hospitals, and little information about which gases were involved in the disaster and what their effects were, large segments of the medical community in Bhopal mounted a herculean effort, beginning in the early morning of December 3. Many would work for the next several days virtually nonstop to try to aid the stricken.

On the first day, 20,000 people crowded into the 1,000-bed Hamidia Hospital alone. Patients were crowded into halls, crammed into wards, lying three and four to a bed. Tents and lean-tos were set up on the hospital grounds to give minimal shelter and comfort to the thousands who couldn't be admitted to the hospital. Because of the impossible overcrowding, many patients were discharged on the verge of death, and others were admitted only when it was too late to save them.

Patients came to the hospitals suffering from a host of afflictions. Doctors reported "devastating" changes in the victims' lungs, including "tracheitis, bronchitis, pulmonary edema and bronchopneumonic changes." According to the Indian Council of Medical Research (ICMR), between eight and ten thousand people were treated at Hamidia Hospital for eye problems on the first day, including for "intense burning of the eyes, profuse lacrimation, photophobia and blepherospasm and visual disturbances."[3] Others suffered from intense gastritis, burning sensations, vomiting, and diarrhea, and many patients lapsed into unconsciousness, asphyxia, and coma.

With little or no knowledge of MIC and its reaction byproducts, doctors were forced to resort to symptomatic treatment (which was all that was prescribed in the available literature from Union Carbide in any event). Patients' eyes were washed out and they were given atrophine to prevent corneal damage. Oxygen and bronchodilators were used to help patients breathe, lasix was given to relieve pulmonary edema, large doses of steroids were injected to combat tissue damage, and in some cases antibiotics were used to guard against secondary infections.

All this was made doubly hard by the short supply of medicines. There was no stockpile of disposable syringes, so needles were used repeatedly, increasing the danger of infection. Of the two steroids being used, hydrocortisone and decadion, there was an inadequate supply of the faster-acting first drug.[4] Nor were there adequate supplies of neosporin, an effective eye medicine. Hamidia had only 100 cylinders of oxygen and literally a handful of respirators – and 20,000 patients with lung damage.[5]

But while the initial medical response had to be ad hoc and could only deal with symptoms, by midday of December 3, some doctors began to understand why many had died so quickly, and so many others were still suffering. They discovered strong evidence that Bhopal had been hit with the same gas used to slaughter millions in German concentration camps: cyanide. MIC is a tremendously lethal gas in its own right, and was the main agent of death in Bhopal, but the revelation of the high probability that cyanide was also involved makes it even clearer that Bhopal had literally been turned into a gas chamber.

Dr. Heeresh Chandra, the head of the Department of Forensic Medicine and Toxicology at Gandhi Medical College, headed up a team from the college that performed 155 autopsies in the first twenty-four hours after the disaster. In each one, the team found striking evidence of cyanide poisoning. The first symptom that alerted Dr. Chandra was the absence of cyanosis – the blue discoloration of the body resulting from deoxygenated blood. Cyanosis might normally be expected in cases of pulmonary asphyxiation, which, on first glance, seemed to be the main effect of the MIC. Instead, the victims' bodies were pinkish, and the venous blood was bright, cherry-red in color, indicating oxygen richness.[6]

This is a classic sign of hydrogen cyanide poisoning. Cyanide inhibits the action of cellular enzymes which are essential links in the transport and use of oxygen in the cell. When these enzymes are prevented from operating, the victims' blood remains bright red, a sign that the tissues have not been able to use the oxygen which remains bound to the hemoglobin in the blood. In the Bhopal victims, some tissue samples contained cyanide residues, and blood pH alkalinity and early rigor mortis also pointed to cyanide poisoning. The cyanide diagnosis also conformed to the manner in which thousands had died. The immediate result of cyanide's blockage of oxygen usage in cells is cellular asphyxiation, to which the cells of the central nervous system are most vulnerable. The result is respiratory failure, convulsions, cardiovascular collapse, loss of control over the bladder and sphincter, and coma – precisely the symptoms of thousands in Bhopal. In fact, the victims had died of respiratory arrest even when neither pulmonary edema nor perforation of lung tissues was found. "Vomiting, convulsions, death is the normal pattern for cyanide poisoning," said Dr. Chandra. Cyanide also explained the extent and rapidity of death. "There is no other poison which can kill people like this," Dr. Chandra commented.[7]

By 3:00 p.m. on December 3, Dr. Chandra made his findings known to the medical authorities in Bhopal, and recommended the use of sodium thiosulphate, a universally recognized antidote for cyanide poisoning.[8] Over the next several days, confirmation of his hypothesis, and recommendations, came from other sources as well, including Union Carbide Corporation itself. On December 5, Dr. Bipin Avashia, the medical director at Carbide's Institute plant, sent a telegram to Bhopal medical personnel on the effects and treatment of MIC exposure, which reads in part: "If cyanide poisoning is suspected use Amyl Nitrite. If no effect – Sod. Nitrite - 0.3 Gms. & Sod. Thiosulphate 12.5 Gms."[9] While this is not an overt admission on his part that there was cyanide poisoning, it is a clear indication that Dr. Avashia was well aware of the possibility.* On December 8, Dr. Max Daunderer, a well-

---

*Dr. Avashia later argued that cyanide was not involved in the disaster. When closely questioned about his telegram by Indian journalists at a December 14

respected clinical toxicologist from West Germany, came to Bhopal. He soon confirmed the cyanide diagnosis and recommended injections of sodium thiosulphate.[10]

Despite these indications of cyanide poisoning, sodium thiosulphate was not administered. Union Carbide's efforts to squelch the cyanide diagnosis began the day after the disaster. On December 4, while stressing it had little knowledge of the accident's causes, Carbide issued a press release stating, "Indications are that the incident involved methyl isocyanate...and not phosgene or cyanide gas."[13] When Warren Anderson, other Carbide officials, and U. S. doctors arrived in India, they told Indian doctors that methyl isocyanate was not to be confused with cyanide; they were two different chemicals and there was no connection between them.[14] Dr. Avashia, a member of the Carbide delegation, said that treatment with sodium thiosulphate was neither necessary nor advisable.[15] Dr. R. M. Bhandare, the medical superintendent at Hamidia, and Dr. N. P. Misra, the dean of the College of Medicine at Gandhi Medical College, also opposed Dr. Chandra's findings, demanding clinical proof of cyanide poisoning before they would authorize the widespread use of sodium thiosulphate.[16]

Dr. Daunderer had brought 50,000 ampules of the drug to India, where it isn't widely available, and administered it to fifty patients, with generally favorable results. But Bhopal's medical establishment prevented him from continuing the treatment and he soon left the country.[17]

The rejection of the cyanide diagnosis and sodium thiosulphate treatment was effectively formalized in a December 13 letter from M. N. Nagu, director of health services for the

---

press conference in Bhopal, Dr. Avashia was evasive. He claimed that he had heard on the radio that cyanide was involved in the gas leak, and so included the information on cyanide.[11] Journalists in Bhopal admit that because of the utter lack of knowledge of MIC prior to the disaster, a number of press reports did mislabel the killer gas "methyl isocyanide" or "methyl isocyanite." But in Dr. Avashia's telegram, his advice on cyanide was clearly in the context of and related to the treatment of MIC exposure. Further, being the medical director at a plant very similar to the one in Bhopal, Avashia would have known not only what the Bhopal plant produced, but that Carbide does not manufacture "methyl isocyanite," or "methyl isocyanide."[12]

Madhya Pradesh government, to Bhopal's doctors. It stated that "under no circumstances shall sodium thiosulphate be given unless it is correctly and conclusively proved in the laboratory that it is cyanide poisoning."[18] While this letter was designed so that it didn't ban sodium thiosulphate outright, its effect was virtually that, because it came directly from the government and imposed conditions for sodium thiosulphate use that were impossible to meet. On December 14, the Indian Council of Medical Research (ICMR) sent a telegram to Bhopal's medical authorities explaining how to administer sodium thiosulphate. This telegram probably would have encouraged the supporters of sodium thiosulphate treatment. But Bhopal's medical authorities didn't release it until three weeks later, in the first week of January, and it was another month before the ICMR directly intervened – confirming the cyanide diagnosis and supporting the use of sodium thiosulphate.[19]

Several arguments were advanced – and are still being advanced – to defend the suppression of this drug. Union Carbide doctors and officials claim that MIC isn't in any way related to cyanide and can't be transformed or metabolized into cyanide.* But the Occupational Safety and Health Administration's "Occupational Health Guideline for Methyl Isocyanate" states that "Toxic gases and vapors (such as hydrogen cyanide, oxides of nitrogen, and carbon monoxide) may be released in a fire involving methyl isocyanate."[20] And Union Carbide now admits that temperatures in MIC tank 610 were probably in excess of 200 degrees C. during the runaway chain reaction; thus a MIC-cyanide transformation was quite possible. (The *Madhya Pradesh Chronicle* reports that confidential Union Carbide manuals in its possession say that thermal decomposition of MIC "may produce hydrogen cyanide," and that such decomposition takes place at 218 degrees C.)[21]

Dr. Misra opposed sodium thiosulphate treatment because there was no "objective" clinical proof of cyanide poisoning.[22] But cyanide is quickly metabolized in the body and quite difficult to

---

*MIC contains all the constituent elements of hydrogen cyanide – carbon, nitrogen, and hydrogen. It should be noted that hydrogen cyanide and "cyanide" are used interchangeably in this book.

detect chemically – for instance in tissue samples – therefore lab findings are generally inconclusive when investigating cyanide poisoning. A toxicology textbook, *Laboratory Diagnosis of Diseases Caused by Toxic Agents,* states, "Hydrogen cyanide is metabolized by the body, and accordingly, it will disappear from the blood. . . Since cyanide is metabolized rapidly, the recognition of chronic intoxication cannot clearly be established. . . The human body has a metabolic mechanism for efficient conversion of small quantities of cyanide into thiocyanate. Accordingly, the first step involved in investigating the possibilities of chronic cyanide intoxication is to establish whether thiocyanate is increased in the blood, urine, or saliva."[23]

"Why do they insist on objective findings when they don't have the means for it?" asked Dr. Chandra. "And what objective findings do they have for the steroids and bronchodilators that they are prescribing?" At the same time, Dr. Chandra and 200 doctors, government officials, and police had been taking sodium thiosulphate from the start – some doctors in order to combat the effects of the gases they had inhaled when performing *post mortems.* The drug improved how they felt and led to measurable improvements in the blood-oxygen levels of 150 doctors, as well as higher levels of thiocyanate in their urine – a sign that cyanide was being neutralized.

But Dr. Misra stated he gave sodium thiosulphate to a number of patients soon after the disaster and "didn't get any encouraging results." Specifically, on the third day after the disaster, he gave sodium thiosulphate to ten patients who died soon afterwards. He admitted, however, that eight of the ten were "very bad" – terminal patients who "would have died anyway."

Since a clear line of treatment was lacking and so many were dying, why not administer sodium thiosulphate, even if one wasn't totally sure of the cyanide diagnosis? Because of the possibility of harmful side effects, some said. What were these? Dr. B. B. L. Mathur, Dean of Gandhi Medical College and one of those who had not supported using the drug, admitted that, according to the literature, "there are no significant adverse reactions" to sodium thiosulphate, but then added that "minor reactions in the nature of some allergic type manifestations" and reactions to the injections themselves were possible.[24] Dr. Misra cited four cases of skin rashes resulting from sodium thiosulphate injections after the disaster. "We can say that the incidence of rashes was approximately five percent," he said. At an ICMR meeting in mid-February, Misra said he had observed adverse reactions, including vomiting, nausea, and fever, in two of the two hundred individuals who had received an injection of sodium thiosulphate.[25] Again, these were minor side effects, which result from the detoxification of the toxins remaining in the body – the so-called "cyanide pool," and pass fairly quickly. In other words, sodium thiosulphate has no serious side effects. "What does it matter if patients are treated with a harmless drug?" asked Dr. S. Sriramachari, the Director of the ICMR Institute of Pathology in New Delhi.[26] And this in a situation where drugs such as steroids, which are much more harmful than sodium thiosulphate, were being given out, as one doctor noted, "like sweets."

Evidence supporting the cyanide hypothesis grew in the months following the disaster. In addition to the studies carried out by Dr. Chandra, the ICMR did a study of forty patients and announced on February 12, 1985, "The results of a double blind controlled study . . . revealed that administration of sodium thiosulphate results in symptomatic improvement and in increased excretion of thiocyanate in the urine . . . indicative of clearance of cyanide-pool from the bodies of persons exposed to the gas in Bhopal." Thiocyanate levels in the urine were reportedly between two and one-half and eight times higher than the highest values in a normal patient. The ICMR also participated in twenty-two autopsies and concurred with Dr. Chandra's findings. It stated, "On the basis of clear-cut results obtained now, the State Government had been advised to administer sodium thiosulphate to the exposed population."[27]

On April 4, 1985, the ICMR stated that follow-up studies had been done on 180 patients who had received sodium thiosulphate injections, indicating an "amelioration of symptoms in a good proportion of cases. No serious adverse effects have been observed."[28]

In January 1985, a special 30-bed hospital was established near the Carbide factory for treatment of some of the victims. The results from sodium thiosulphate treatment were encouraging.

One doctor working there said in late February that the drug had been given to over 1,000 people. "Sodium thiosulphate is helpful in breaking the cycle of repeated illness, the cycle of people coming and getting treated and then coming back again for another treatment for the same illness. Just ask the patients how they feel about it."[29]

There is still debate in India on precisely what exploded out of tank 610 and how it affected its victims, including the possible synergistic effects of the half dozen or so toxic gases that were probably involved (effects greater than the simple sum of those of the gases involved). Because MIC is so lethal and also attacks the nervous system, Dr. Chandra says it isn't out of the question that MIC itself produced some of the cyanide-like reactions evident in gas victims. Dr. Sriramachari feels that both MIC and cyanide may have been involved: cyanide being responsible for the initial, massive deaths and the cyanate radical in MIC for the chronic, cyanide-type poisoning that doctors are now witnessing in the gas-affected.

But at this point, nearly all agree that cyanide or cyanide-like toxins were involved in the disaster. Dr. Misra says that the ICMR had conclusively proved that the exothermic reaction in tank 610 had led "to the liberation of three types of gases which are very poisonous besides methyl isocyanate. One is hydrocyanic acid, which can get absorbed and produce cyanide poisoning, another is nitrous oxide, and carbon monoxide. They do not allow oxygen to be delivered at the level of the tissues. . .the tissues get asphyxiated."

But despite the growing evidence and agreement, controversy in India around the cyanide/sodium thiosulphate issue continues. Leading doctors in Bhopal and the Madhya Pradesh government say that there never was a cyanide controversy within official circles, and that the sodium thiosulphate treatment wasn't suppressed.[30] Dr. Misra, while now agreeing that hydrocyanic acid left tank 610, still contends that there is no evidence to support the view that gas victims are now suffering from chronic-type cyanide poisoning – caused either by cyanide directly or MIC itself. He adds, despite all the evidence to the contrary, that there is no "objective" evidence that sodium thiosulphate helps the afflicted.[31]

The Medico Friends Circle, a volunteer group of Indian doctors which has studied the situation in Bhopal, stated in mid-February 1985, "Even today clear guidelines for its [sodium thiosulphate] administration to patients have not been issued, nor is the injection yet being made available in the quantity required for massive detoxification of the affected population."[32] As of August 1985, sodium thiosulphate treatment was still highly inadequate. The ICMR has recommended its use, but has not implemented a mass detoxification program.

The government's inaction has generated considerable anger, especially in the most heavily affected slums. Many have complained that the medication prescribed by most doctors hasn't helped at all. On March 24, 1985, 150 women demonstrated outside the government's thirty-bed clinic, demanding proper treatment, including sodium thiosulphate injections.[33] In mid-March, when members of the Medico Friends Circle and the Bhopal Zahreeli Gas Kand Sangharsh Morcha (Bhopal Poisonous Gas Episode Struggle Front—hereafter referred to as the Morcha), organized a mobile exhibit to teach gas-affected slum dwellers about the special problems of women as well as about sodium thiosulphate treatment, government doctors tried to undercut their efforts by arguing that slum dwellers couldn't be taught to save urine samples that are necessary for testing, after sodium thiosulphate injections are administered. A group of women then confronted them with bottles of urine, and demanded they be given the injections.[34]

On June 3, 1985, several volunteer organizations, working independently of the Indian government to bring relief to gas victims, established the People's Health Clinic on Union Carbide premises in Bhopal. The clinic's purpose was to provide free medical help − including thiosulphate injections − to gas victims. On the night of June 24, 1984, the police raided the clinic on grounds of "illegal occupation," arrested and beat nine volunteers, including three doctors and a medical student, and confiscated the clinic's records and supplies.[35]

As for Union Carbide, in late February 1985, the company sent two of its doctors to India, one a former chemical warfare expert at England's Chemical Defense Establishment at Porton Down and an authority on cyanide poisoning.[36] They gave medical personnel in Bhopal technical documents, some of which dealt with the diagnosis of cyanide poisoning. In light of the company's unequivocal denial of cyanide being involved in the disaster, this was probably more an effort to investigate the situation in Bhopal and maintain a "helpful" posture than to seriously examine the cyanide thesis.

On March 15, 1985, Union Carbide announced that it would "sponsor a metabolism study in animals to evaluate whether a single, large exposure to methyl isocyanate can, for example, lead to the generation of cyanide." The company cited as its reason for the study "reports from India that a number of deaths did not appear to be associated with methyl isocyanate–related overexposures, but rather were suggestive of cyanide poisoning."[37] But such a study is simply a face-saving diversion from the real issue. Doctors in India argue that MIC was converted into cyanide during the reaction in tank 610, not metabolized into cyanide within the bodies of the victims. As of August 1985, the corporation was holding to its position that cyanide was not involved in the disaster, and Dr. Avashia still maintained that "there's no justification" for sodium thiosulphate treatment.[38]

But most significantly, Union Carbide's report of March 20, 1985, based on 500 laboratory experiments utilizing tank residues, supposedly replicated the chemistry involved in the December 2–3 chain reaction with a "high degree of probability." The chemical residue in tank 610 was closely examined. Yet the report contains nothing about which chemicals, in addition to MIC, left the tank. The report simply concludes that "Approximately 54,000 pounds of unreacted MIC left Tank 610 together with approximately 26,000 pounds of reaction products." Since they had conducted 500 experiments, had access to tank residues, and claimed to recreate the deadly chemistry in tank 610, it would be reasonable to think that Union Carbide might have some notion of which reaction products, in addition to MIC, enveloped Bhopal, and that this would be of considerable interest to doctors and victims. But Union Carbide has said nothing.[39]

In a similar vein, the U.S. press blacked out the cyanide story for more than three months after the disaster, long after it was the subject of intense discussion in Indian government and medical circles and in the Indian press. The blackout was lifted briefly when a handful of articles appeared, mainly in April 1985, but apparently with the aim of trying to discount the evidence of cyanide poisoning.

An article in the April 1 *Wall Street Journal*, on the problems confronting the surviving gas victims, mentions the cyanide controversy and claims that blood tests have shown no evidence of cyanide poisoning.[40] An April 10 article in the *New York Times* quotes Dr. Misra as saying there is still no conclusive proof of cyanide poisoning. It states that a number of U.S. experts have denigrated the cyanide thesis because MIC can't be converted into cyanide, and because there's no "rationale" for treating patients with sodium thiosulphate so long after possible cyanide exposure. The article also cites conflicting testimony from *three* patients, and sums up that the evidence for cyanide poisoning is "inconclusive."[41] A February 11, 1985 article in *Chemical and Engineering News* states, "But U.S. scientists have characterized such reports of cyanide poisoning as 'highly questionable' and 'probably spurious.' They have criticized the analytical methods that were used to determine cyanide. And they note that there's no known metabolic pathway that converts isocyanate into cyanide."[42]

None of these articles mentions the widely known and reported studies in India, cited above, that contained evidence of both cyanide poisoning and the efficacy of the sodium thio-sulphate treatment, or refers to Dr. Chandra and his findings. They also fail to explain that Indian doctors don't argue that MIC was metabolized into cyanide within the victims' bodies, but rather that cyanide was a product of the reaction in tank 610.

The great bulk of evidence in this cyanide controversy points to a coverup which can't be written off as mere medical pedantry or conservatism, or a product of uncertainties surrounding the events of the disaster. It would seem to be a conscious suppression of the truth, with further cruel effects for the victims.

Why was this done? Prior to December 3, 1984, MIC was a relatively unknown chemical, and therefore didn't have the connotations that cyanide evokes. Any association of MIC with cyanide, any public perception that MIC and cyanide are somehow linked, could lead to multimillion-dollar losses for Union Carbide – which manufactures two-thirds of the world's

MIC[43] − and the other big chemical concerns, including Dupont, Dow, and FMC, which manufacture or use it. It would underscore Union Carbide's criminal negligence concerning matters of safety and health in Bhopal; it would deepen public mistrust and fear of the chemical industry generally; and, because of cyanide's historical "uses," it would bring home more acutely than the unknown MIC the stark reality behind claims of how foreign capital "brings progress" to the Third World.

People in the Indian government and medical establishment, including some doctors in Bhopal, went along with this suppression and coverup for deeper reasons than the widely reported links, nepotistic and otherwise, between some of them and Union Carbide.* These people represent sectors of Indian society which are closely tied to and dependent upon foreign capital, and which view continued close relations as essential to their favored economic position and social and political influence.

Few Indian doctors, including those in Bhopal, knew anything about MIC, or its possible connections with cyanide. In the disaster's aftermath, many doctors struggled to learn the truth about which gases were afflicting and killing thousands; some others chose to accept Union Carbide's word for it when it said that cyanide had nothing to do with the disaster.

As for the Indian government, the situation is complex, as reflected in the differing positions that government doctors have taken on the cyanide question. Some officials are more nationalistically inclined, and some favor a tilt to the East rather than the West. The Indian government may also have other reasons for covering up the cyanide diagnosis and helping to suppress a promising line of treatment. But in this and other matters,

*For instance, it has been widely reported in the Indian press that the dean of the College of Medicine at Gandhi Medical College, Dr. N.P. Misra, a key figure in the suppression of the cyanide diagnosis, had close links with Union Carbide. Dr. Misra, whose business card says he is the personal physician to the Governor of the state of Madhya Pradesh, denies having any special relationship with Union Carbide, but he had been informed by Union Carbide of some of the dangers of MIC − one of the few doctors in Bhopal or India who had. When asked why he didn't alert the medical community of the potential danger, Misra replied, "This is not the only compound about which you do not know. . . . There are thousands of other potentially dangerous compounds about which you do not know today, as you did not know about MIC."

the Indian government has generally worked to downplay the extent and seriousness of the disaster, in an effort not only to hide its own bungling and culpability but to preserve social order and, most importantly, its links with foreign capital.[44]

Even today, after numerous studies and considerable experience have corroborated the cyanide diagnosis and sodium thiosulphate treatment, the efforts to suppress them continue. In the U.S., Union Carbide and the major media have seen to it that this aspect of the Bhopal disaster has remained virtually unknown.

The medical coverup in Bhopal doesn't end with the probability of cyanide poisoning. Bhopal was the most massive industrial disaster in history, but the full dimension of the human toll in deaths, injuries and crippling disabilities remains obscured and confused by a host of conflicting diagnoses from various experts; the appalling lack of information on the effects of MIC and its reaction products; the secrecy surrounding official medical records; and most importantly, efforts by Union Carbide in particular, and some in the Indian government and medical establishment, to downplay the extent of the medical catastrophe.

The actual number of people who initially died in this disaster has itself become a political football. This is due principally to the efforts of Union Carbide, the Indian government, and others to minimize the proportions of the massacre. It also reflects conditions in a Third World country like India, where achieving an accurate count of those who die in a disaster can be difficult. For example, many of the Bhopal victims were homeless laborers, with no relatives to claim their bodies and make sure their deaths were recorded, or to initiate a search for them if they were missing.

As of August 1985, the Indian government had confirmed that 1,754 people had died in the disaster, and it estimates another two to three hundred may be added as new victims are discovered and more people die from the after-effects of the gassing.* But this figure is clearly low. People in Bhopal, and

---

*The government figure is a compilation of the number of confirmed deaths from

throughout India, feel that anywhere from five to fifteen thousand perished. In fact, the government estimate is so widely disbelieved that officials don't attempt to contradict the higher figures appearing in the Indian press – although even in private they come up with the very conservative number of about 2,500. Bhopal residents reported that they counted on their own over 1,000 bodies on the morning after the disaster. People living near the Carbide plant have told volunteer medical and relief groups they saw the Indian army cart off dead bodies by the truckload – bodies which were never accounted for. One Indian journalist reports that over 4,000 burial shrouds were sold in Bhopal the day after the gas leak.[45]

People also argue that many residents who fled the city to outlying areas, only to die there, were never counted. (Forty thousand people were treated in the twenty-two districts outside of Bhopal, giving some indication of how many affected people fled the city.)[46] Doctors at Hamidia note that relatives of many victims simply took the bodies before any death certificate could be issued and buried them on their own.

The chaos of the first day and the bureaucratic approach of the Indian authorities has also made accurate record-keeping difficult. The Morcha, a volunteer group which has studied the medical effects of the Bhopal disaster, found that in Muslim graveyards five bodies were being buried in each grave, yet only one death certificate was generally issued. In a partial survey of the J.P. Nagar shanty colony, across the street from Union Carbide, the Morcha found that of 231 reported deaths, only 92 death certificates had been issued.[47]

Medical surveys also support the contention that the number of deaths is much higher than official government estimates. Doctors from Bombay studied a moderately affected community of 10,000, two kilometers from the factory, and found there were between 150 and 170 deaths. If this percentage held for the entire 200,000 affected (some more and some less than this community), the dead would total 3,200.[48] The Morcha's survey of slums close to Union Carbide revealed a death rate of seven

---

hospitals, crematoriums, and burial grounds in Bhopal, as well as reported deaths in outlying areas where people had fled.

percent, which if extended over the 65,000 who live in the most severely affected area, would mean that over 4,500 died.[49]

Meanwhile, Union Carbide has said that at least for the time being, it is going along with the Indian government's death figures, although the corporation's outside counsel told the *Washington Post* that, for legal purposes, the corporation only accepts the 1,408 deaths officially recorded at Bhopal hospitals.[50] As for the U.S. media, it has generally discounted the much higher estimates and reported that between 2,000 and 2,500 people died.

A battle has also developed over the dimensions of the aftereffects on those who survived. One Union Carbide memo, dated November 23, 1983, lists the effects of various chemicals the company produces. Its most dangerous rating, number four, includes substances that "are known human carcinogens; result in mutagenesis, teratogenesis, or fertility impairment in humans; result in irreversible central nervous system disturbances; result in cumulating long-term organ toxicity that is irreversible; are predominantly fast acting and can produce major injury; and have exposure limits of < 5 ppm [less than 5 parts per million]." MIC, chloroform, and phosgene are all rated number four by Carbide.[51]

Yet just ten days after the disaster, because eye and skin damage appeared less extensive than expected, a number of U.S. doctors associated with Union Carbide, along with some Indian doctors, proclaimed that victims would suffer few after-effects. A Union Carbide press release on December 21, 1984, quotes Dr. Avashia as saying, "It is unlikely that there will be any permanent blindness," and that of the surviving victims with pulmonary edema, many improved within ten days and local physicians expect that those still showing symptoms would improve within three weeks.[52] These optimistic predictions were bolstered by Carbide's contention that on contact with water or water vapor in the atmosphere, MIC degraded into harmless chemicals. Some doctors concluded from this that many victims may not have inhaled excessive quantities of MIC, since much of it was quickly neutralized, or that MIC would not have long-lasting effects because it would be neutralized by water in the body.[53]

Dr. Peter Halberg, an opthalmologist who accompanied Dr.

Avashia and Warren Anderson to India, agreed that few would suffer permanent damage to their eyes. He stated that most eye damage had been on the superficial layer of the cornea, which would regenerate in a few days. A small percentage of victims had injuries in deeper layers of the eye, and their vision could be impaired in varying degrees. He also ruled out total blindness, arguing that those few cases of total vision loss could be cured by a corneal transplant.[54] Dr. Hans Weill, a pulmonary specialist, was more cautious because there was no precedent for MIC poisoning. However, he compared the gas victims to those exposed to chlorine gas in Florida, saying that in the Florida case, most of the victims did not show any lasting ill effects. He also stated that fetuses probably wouldn't be affected by the gassing, nor would it produce genetic disorders in the unborn; and that the liver, kidney, and heart would not be affected by the gas directly, but only in cases where the organs couldn't get sufficient oxygen.[55] The headline on a December 20, 1984 *New York Times* article captured the essence of this trend of thought among U.S. and Indian doctors: "Few Lasting Health Effects Found Among India Gas-Leak Survivors."

The reality for gas victims in Bhopal stands in grim contrast to these pronouncements, and like the cyanide poisoning, is a subject which the U.S. media has largely ignored. According to government doctors, some 200,000 people were exposed to the gases, over 65,000 inhaled large quantities, and 170,000 were treated by doctors in Bhopal, most on an outpatient basis.

Of these, Dr. Misra estimates that approximately "5,000 were severely affected . . . they are going to get lung problems in the future no matter what treatment you give them because if the lung tissue is destroyed it cannot be replaced." He noted that exposure to MIC can sensitize the lung tissue, exacerbating the tuberculosis, chronic bronchitis, and emphysema from which many impoverished slum dwellers already suffer. He also said that as of mid-February 1985, 10,000 patients were still undergoing treatment, between 1,000 and 1,500 were visiting hospitals in Bhopal each day, many of them gas-affected, and that 2,000 were still suffering from "visual impairment," although he felt they would improve over time. As of August 1985, the Indian government estimated that 17,000 people had suffered irreparable damage from the disaster.[56]

But studies by a number of doctors and volunteer organizations paint a far grimmer picture of the depth and extent of the ailments. A group of doctors from Bombay's KEM hospital studied 120 middle-class victims (whose post-disaster physical condition can't be attributed to poverty), moderately affected by the gassing. They found that only 4 to 5 percent of their lung x-rays were normal, and, of the 95 percent who showed damage, only 10 percent of these patients' lungs were improving. Dr. S. R. Kamat, a leader of the survey, criticized doctors in Bhopal for underestimating the amount of lung damage in gas victims.

The same team also studied a community of 10,000 people living two kilometers from the railway station. Government doctors generally argue that the gas damaged only the eyes and lungs, with other organs such as the liver, kidney, and brain either unaffected or affected only as a result of hypoxia (lack of oxygen).* The Bombay group found not only lung and eye damage, but also a significant minority who were acutely ill and suffering from lack of control of their urinary function, nose and throat problems, diarrhea, vomiting, and abdominal pains. Dr. Kamat also felt there was a strong possibility of serious neurological effects resulting from the massive exposure. He cited as evidence a 1976 study of the effects on 35 English firemen exposed to toluene diisocyanate, a chemical closely related to MIC.

A December–January 1985 Morcha survey of the most badly affected slums is also revealing. Surveying 812 families, a total population of 4,000 in six slums, Morcha members found that 3,590, or nearly 90 percent of those surveyed, were still suffering ill effects from the gassing, including listlessness, gastritis, chest pains, abdominal pain and swelling, skin diseases and eruptions, breathlessness, blurred vision, exhaustion, and gynecological disorders. Of the 1,152 who had worked prior to the disaster, 881

---

*In interviews, Drs. Misra, Mathur, and Ishwar Das, the additional chief secretary in charge of coordinating health and relief services in Madhya Pradesh, all contended that the effects of the gassing were basically confined only to the lungs and eyes of the victims. On December 26, 1984, Dr. Das stated officially, "No organ of the body has been affected except the eye and the lung: There is not a single case of kidney, liver or nervous system damage."[57]

– over 75 percent – were incapacitated and unable to return to work.[58]

During the spring of 1985, between 500 and 600 people were visiting the special thirty-bed hospital daily. Doctors there conservatively estimate that 40 percent are suffering from gas exposure. Their ailments include breathlessness, burning in the eyes, severe pain in their chests, heaviness in their heads, and intestinal distress. A survey by the Medico Friends Circle found, in addition to widespread eye and lung damage, that "people also suffer on a large scale from gastritis, fever and psychological stress of varying severity."[59]

One of the most disputed aspects of the disaster has been its effect on women. Government doctors have said virtually nothing on the question of the general effects on women, and vigorously argue that there has been no appreciable rise in the number of spontaneous abortions and stillbirths. A July 16, 1985 *New York Times* article – the only article the *Times* has printed on this issue – quotes the public health minister of Madhya Pradesh as saying that thirty-six pregnant women spontaneously aborted and six gave birth to deformed babies after the toxic gas leak. Autopsies on twenty-seven other stillborn babies also indicate the possibility that they died because of MIC.[60] But studies by volunteer medical groups and others reveal that these figures are very low.

In January 1985, Tappan Bose, an Indian filmmaker, said that in a survey of 1,900 homes, he found over 100 spontaneous abortions and 22 stillbirths in the wake of the gas leak.[61] The Medico Friends Circle report noted that "Women have suffered from abortions, stillbirths, diminished fetal movements, suppression of lactation, abnormal vaginal discharge and menstrual disturbances."[62] Dr. Sharma Narain, a member of the Medico Friends team, added that while women's problems were being officially denied, "some sympathetic doctors report seeing a very high rate of spontaneous abortions, and a very high rate of 'missed' abortions – dead fetuses – along with hard, very tense uteruses in which the blood circulation is constricted, and heavy and more frequent menstruation."[63]

A study by Dr. Rani Bang, a gynecologist, uncovered evidence of devastating gynecological changes among gas-affected women. With help from other medical volunteers, she examined 114 women in two of the severely affected slums, J. P. Nagar and Kazi Camp, in early March 1985. These results were compared to those from a control group of 104 women living in two other slums with similar social characteristics which were either unaffected or very minimally affected by the December 3 gas leak. Pelvic examinations were conducted on 72 women in the gas-affected slums and 52 women in the unaffected slums.

The differences between the two groups were startling. Ninety percent of the gas-affected women had leucorrhea, a profuse, thick, whitish-yellow discharge from the vagina; only 27 percent of the unaffected did. Seventy-nine percent of the gas-affected had pelvic inflammatory diseases versus 27 percent in the unaffected group, and 75 percent of the gas victims suffered from cervical erosion and/or endocervicitis compared to 44 percent in the control group. Thirty-one percent studied in the two affected slums exhibited excessive menstrual bleeding, compared to 1.2 percent in the unaffected slums. There were some complaints of lactation suppression. Seven women had spontaneous abortions following the gas leak and four delivered stillborn babies. Dr. Bang notes that these and other gynecological problems are unnoticed and unattended by the medical establishment, and need immediate medical relief and research.[64]

The impact on the fetuses of pregnant women, particularly those women who were in their first trimester when exposed to the gases, is an especially sharp question. Drs. Mira Sadgopal, Rani Bang and a number of others have urged that abortion be actively considered by such women, to prevent deformed babies or harm to the affected mothers. While some government doctors agree privately that such abortions may be wise, the government has taken no action to inform women of these possible dangers and the abortion option.

As of summer 1985, the horrendous medical conditions of the victims had not abated. One former resident who visited Bhopal in June and July reports that between 50,000 and 60,000 still suffer chronic and long-term lung damage, and most are unable to work or exert themselves for any length of time. Many victims also suffer from severe psychological trauma brought on by the disaster.[65] In late June, the Morcha's Anil Sadgopal stated that people in Bhopal were still suffering from fatigue, kidney failure, and bleeding; 95 percent of the seriously affected women had disturbed menstrual cycles; and there had been hundreds of spontaneous abortions and stillbirths.[66]

Union Carbide's actions have contributed to the difficulty in determining exactly what continues to ail tens of thousands in Bhopal. One factor is the uncertainty about just what combination of gases exploded from tank 610. Added to this is the fact that Union Carbide was using massive quantities of a toxic chemical, MIC, about which little is known, and for which there is no antidote. This is a common phenomenon in the chemical industry, where it is estimated that 80 percent of the 60,000 chemicals now in use are never tested for toxic and carcinogenic effects.[67]

This ignorance has been compounded by the fact that Union Carbide hasn't been forthcoming with whatever information on MIC it does have. While it has publicly proclaimed its willingness to share information with medical officials in Bhopal, those officials claim to have received little help from Carbide. "In the beginning we did get a couple of telex messages, but they were not very helpful, and since then they have not volunteered any information so far as the management of these patients is concerned," said Dr. Das.[68] Even *Chemical and Engineering News* writes that "Union Carbide toxicologists may have the best information on MIC toxicity around, but they're treating it like a trade secret."[69]

While holding back information about MIC and its various reaction products that could give a clearer picture of the medical implications of the disaster, and without any substantial contact with the victims in Bhopal, Union Carbide is contending that the number of injuries has been wildly exaggerated. Again the company is doing something of a two-step on this question. The corporation says that at this point it is not contesting the Indian government's injury figures, although a press spokesman did add that a lot of what is now appearing in the press is "speculation." "Something could look long-term and then again it could clear up fairly fast."[70] Meanwhile, its counsel told the *Washington Post* that based on computer analysis that found repetitions on the lists of those who had filed suit against Union Carbide, the company feels that the real numbers are a "small fraction" of what some lawyers and the Indian government claim. "Someone in Bhopal that might have smelled gas and felt bad was not significantly affected," he said. "There were people who fled their homes; there were people who were upset that night. There may have been people who went to first aid because they had felt nausea or felt ill and then left."[71]

As for the U.S. press, aside from a few December 1984 articles on the medical situation in Bhopal and the *New York Times* article in July 1985 cited earlier – all of which found things brighter than originally feared – it hasn't engaged in much coverage. In late March and early April, when there was no denying the continuing disabilities crippling thousands, the *New York Times* and the *Wall Street Journal* each carried one article on the situation.[72] At the same time, the "personal ordeal" of Warren Anderson merited a special three-page spread in the Sunday, May 19, 1985 *New York Times*.[73]

The actions of the Indian government have also complicated the medical situation in Bhopal. A veil of secrecy has been clamped over all but the most general medical information. Detailed medical information and autopsy findings are unavailable. When volunteer doctors visited government clinics and hospitals, they found that patients' charts were not available.

Government officials and doctors insist that it is simply standard medical practice to withhold detailed medical information. But they also admit that India's Central Bureau of Investigation did advise them "not to give every bit of information to the press," and that some information could create public panic. "Some people tried to come out prematurely with half-hearted information," Dr. Mathur said. "This information really did not help the public, it scared them."

Government doctors also bend over backward to make the point that many of the ailments afflicting gas victims, and even the deaths recorded in Bhopal hospitals, may or may not be gas-related. Dr. Abhay Bang, a member of the Medico Friends Circle from Hyderabad, argues that this is a convenient way to cover up the dimensions of the continuing horror gripping Bhopal. With limited equipment and knowledge of the specific effects of the gases involved in the disaster, and because a number of the effects of the gassing resemble other physical ailments, it is often difficult for doctors in the field to conclusively diagnose a patient as a gas victim, he explained. But despite this difficulty, Dr. Bang points out, some doctors are simply assuming "that ailments are psychological or people are faking it to get compensation."[74] The *Indian Express* reports that people seeking readmission to hospitals with recurring ailments have been dismissed as asthma or bronchitis cases instead of acknowledging that their ailments have arisen because of inhaling MIC.[75] It would not be surprising if Union Carbide used this argument should the Bhopal case ever come to court.

Some doctors have attributed victims' lung complaints to poverty-induced tuberculosis. "You know how these people live," is a refrain one hears all too often in Bhopal. Indeed, one of the appalling aspects of the whole disaster is that the victims' poverty and abysmal living conditions are making recovery from the effects of the gassing all the more difficult.

The photos on the following pages were taken by the author, with the exception of those on pages 95 through 101, which are courtesy *The Hitavada.*

J. P. Nagar shanty colony in the shadow of UCC's Bhopal plant

Gas victims who had described the night of horror and the aftermath

Naffeem Bano—found alive among the dead at the mortuary

Child victim with some of the medicines given her family

Gas victims of J. P. Nagar — this child's leg was paralyzed

93

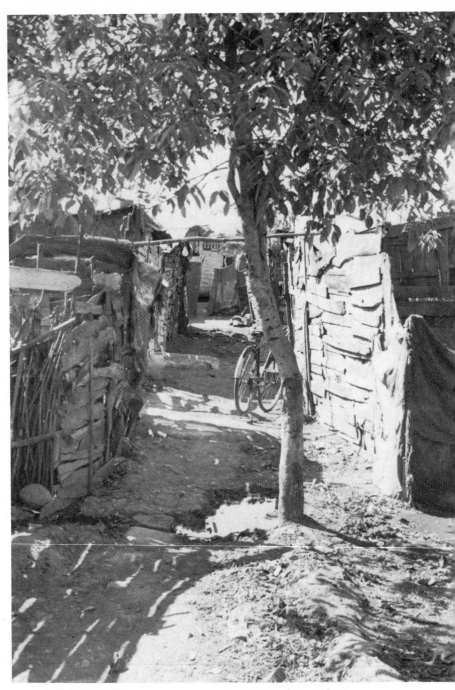

J. P. Nagar alleyway, a narrow escape route for residents

MIC unit at Bhopal plant.

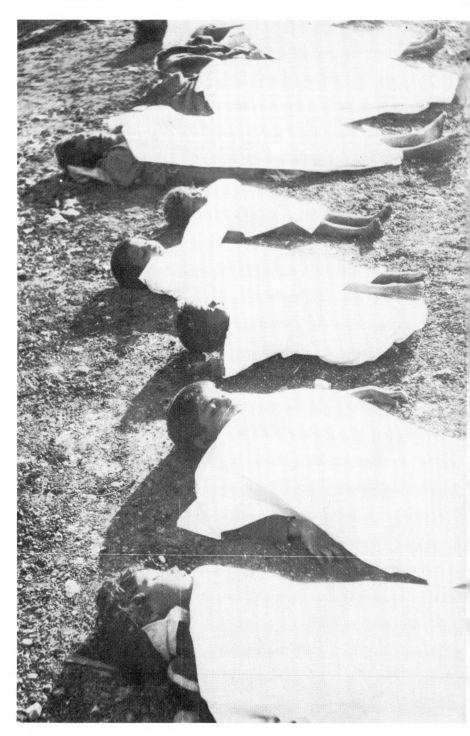

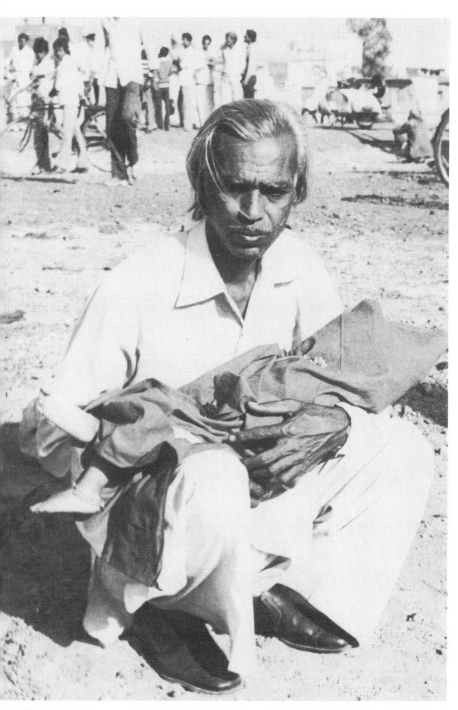

The victims

Clearing the streets of the dead animals

Funeral pyres

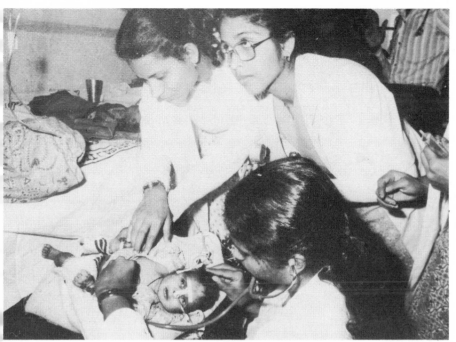

Medical care in the immediate aftermath

Victims awaiting treatment

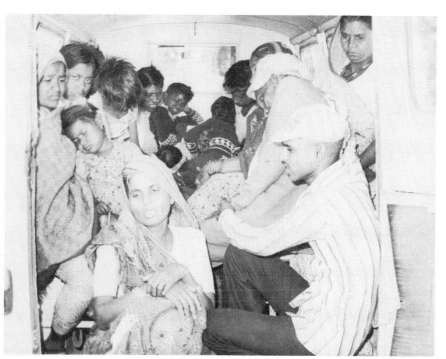

Going to a hospital

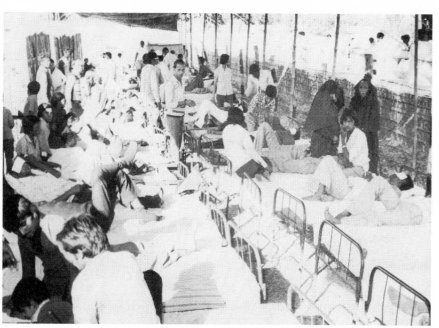

A clinic set up in the wake of disaster

February 16 demonstration winds through streets of Bhopal

February 16 demonstration

*February 16
demonstration*

Women from the shanty colonies at February 16 demonstration

5 | Reaping the Benefits

With funeral pyres still smoldering in Bhopal, some in the U.S. argued that one must look beyond Bhopal to the larger picture. The cloud of toxic fumes that suffocated one Indian city should not be allowed to obscure the overall benefits foreign capital and companies like Union Carbide bring to the Third World.

For example, the *Wall Street Journal* editorialized, "... with recriminations flying, it is worthwhile to remember that the Union Carbide insecticide plant and the people surrounding it were there for compelling reasons. India's agriculture had been thriving, bringing a better life to millions of rural people, and partly because of the use of modern agricultural technology that includes applications of insect killers.... Indians need technology. Calcutta-style scenes of human deprivation can be replaced as fast as the country imports the benefits of the West's industrial revolution and market economics."[1]

Warren Anderson declared that "without the technologies and the capital that multinationals help to introduce, developing countries would have little hope of eradicating poverty and hunger. In India alone, it's been estimated that pesticides save about 10 percent of the annual food crop, enough to feed over 70 million people."[2] A U.S. doctor told the *New York Times*, "Of those people killed, half would not have been alive today if it weren't for that plant and the modern health standards made possible by wide use of pesticides."[3]

But this is not an abstract issue of the use of pesticides. The point isn't technology itself, nor even that a useful technological development can have undesirable consequences. The question is what are the real costs and benefits of such technological innovation and on what basis is such an evaluation made.

To begin with, it is critical to examine under what conditions and with what impact technology is introduced into India and the rest of the Third World. Technology may not be "alive," but neither is it "neutral" because it is introduced under and reinforces certain definite social relationships – between the owners and consumers of the technology, and between people in the society in which it is applied. Time after time, country after country, the evidence shows that such technology strengthens the highly lopsided relation of economic and political domination that prevails between developed countries that export it and its Third World purchasers. Rather than being a direct pathway to progress, it creates new forms of oppression, along with preserving many of the old. Instead of being the key to a "better life" for these countries, it actually perpetuates the poverty and misery, the backwardness that Union Carbide and others target as the source of disasters like Bhopal.

In the early 1960s, the "Green Revolution" was started in India under the auspices of the Ford Foundation.* The heart of the plan was agricultural modernization through the promotion of capitalist farming methods and increased use of modern inputs such as high-yielding seed varieties (HYVs), farm machinery, fertilizers, and pesticides.

Indian agricultural production has grown as a result of the Green Revolution. Since 1965 the area sown with high-yield varieties has gone from nothing to over fifty million hectares, the amount of irrigated land has doubled, fertilizer consumption has

---

*At approximately the same time, the U.S. was sponsoring the "White Revolution" in Iran and the Alliance for Progress in Latin America. While somewhat broader in scope than the "Green Revolution," all of these had the same goal of stabilizing certain strategically important countries or regions and creating new investment opportunities for Western capital through stimulating Third World growth in agriculture.

increased over sixfold, pesticide use over tenfold, and the number of tractors has jumped from 53 thousand to 367 thousand.[4] Agricultural output rose over 2.5 times in the decade of the '70s, and during 1984 India's foodgrain production rose to an alltime high of 151 million tons.[5] But such statistics mask the overall impact that the Green Revolution has had upon India. Although the development and spread of capitalism in Indian agriculture has been spectacular, substantial sections of the countryside are still characterized by extremely backward semifeudal methods of production and social relationships.* The gap between the modernized and semifeudal agricultural sectors has been greatly widened, and overall there is an increasingly distorted agrarian system – marked by slowing rates of growth, heightened dependence on foreign capital needed for agricultural inputs, and continued malnutrition and starvation among the Indian people.†

This "revolution" is predicated upon the increased use of modern inputs to increase production – in fact, it has been called a "revolution in inputs" in India. But these inputs are available and useful only to those with the capital to purchase them and enough land to make them economical. In India, 22 percent of rural families own no land, and 47 percent own less than an acre. These families and millions of other marginal holders are in no position to afford or utilize modern inputs. Only a small percentage – some estimate as low as 3 or 4 percent – of the richest

*Even in areas of more intensive capitalization and development of agriculture and especially other sectors of the economy most transformed by capitalism, all the aspects of feudalism in the superstructure and the relationships of Indian society (for example the still rigid caste system) have by no means been eliminated, but have been incorporated into a more modern system of exploitation.

†Some people argue that although the situation in India today remains bad, it is nonetheless improving because of programs like the Green Revolution. It is true that the average life expectancy has increased from slightly over 30 years in the 1940s, and that infant mortality has dropped by 20 percent in the same period. The kind of massive famines, which took twenty million lives between 1850 and 1900, or as many as three million as recently as 1943, no longer generally occur. But average life expectancy in India is still only 50 years, compared to 74 in the U.S., and 127 out of every thousand Indian babies born die at birth – ten times greater than the U.S. infant mortality rate, and Indian death and infant mortality rates are no longer declining. So it is not a matter – at least not for the great majority of India's impoverished masses – of "slow and steady progress."[6]

farmers are in a position to do so fully.[7] For example, 96 percent of the tractors in India are owned by the 4 percent of Indian landowners with holdings of over twenty-five acres.[8] And these farmers often receive the bulk of available financial support from the state and private banks because of their greater efficiency. Thus wealth is increasingly concentrated in the hands of those farmers who are able to afford modern inputs; this minority in turn uses this new wealth and power to appropriate more land, which in turn puts them in a better position to capitalize on this technology. These wealthier farmers often increase their output, and profit, by simply driving poor tenant farmers off the land, or denying them tenancy rights, and cultivating the land themselves with modern methods and wage labor. In 1969 there were 40,000 eviction suits against sharecroppers in the state of Bihar and 80,000 in the state of Karnatika.[9] One study on farm size in Punjab revealed that mechanized farms grew an average of 240 percent during one three-year period in the 1960s, mainly because landlords cultivated land they had previously rented out. Between 1961 and 1971 the number of agricultural laborers increased by 70 percent (over 20 million), while the number of farmers decreased by 16 percent (15 million).[10]

The large number of small holders who still retain either land or tenancy rights remain locked into a traditional, semifeudal mode of production, and find themselves increasingly unable to compete with the richer, more efficient farmers. Often sharecropping divisions have been shifted in favor of the landlord – due to his increased "technological" contribution to the harvest – from the traditional fifty-fifty arrangement to 70 percent of the crop for the landlord and 30 percent for the tenant. Also, in some areas tenants are paid in cash. In a country like India, this can mean depriving tenants of food by enabling landlords to hoard and speculate on food supplies. And those who now work as agricultural laborers have been cut off from any connection with even subsistence farming.[11]

This combination of outright evictions and increasing rural impoverishment has forced millions of peasants to look for work in India's burgeoning cities, whose population has doubled in the past twenty years.[12] However, the urban industrial and commercial sectors are unable to absorb those streaming off the land because of the distorted and disarticulated development of the overall economy. Thus urban slums swell and the "Calcutta-style scenes of human deprivation" that the *Wall Street Journal* claims to abhor are created. In Bombay, India's richest metropolis and a center of commerce and finance, fully half of the city's 8.75 million people – many of whom are recent immigrants from rural areas – live in slums, and 500,000 live "on the pavement" – without homes. In Bhopal, thousands crowded into makeshift shanties in the deadly shadow of Union Carbide's pesticide factory.[13]

Uncontrolled urban overcrowding and the distorted development of the urban areas are also major contributors to the diseases ravaging India. A critical problem is the lack of clean water and adequate sewage systems. Only 47 percent of the urban population is covered with adequate excreta disposal systems; a third, some 50 million people, have no access to latrines of any kind; and the number of urban dwellers who receive an uninterrupted supply of water has actually declined since 1970 (this is important since interruptions in water pressure lead to negative pressure within water pipes, drawing in contaminants). The Center for Science and the Environment in New Delhi estimates that between 90 and 100 percent of the urban population in nine of India's twenty-two states receives water only intermittently. This contributes to the incidence of filariasis (elephantiasis), which affects 15 million people in India. The population at risk from this disease has risen from 25 million in 1963 to 236 million by 1976. Hepatitis has also been increasing dramatically in most Indian cities. And simple diarrhea, caused by contaminated water and worsened by malnutrition, kills 1.5 million children every year in India, and "constitutes a permanent epidemic in the country."[14]

Even while millions are forced into these urban slums, nearly 500 million people – over 70 percent of the population of India – live in rural areas where the accumulation of wealth by a handful is paralleled by the deepening impoverishment of the vast majority. There, the average family exists on 43 cents a day; half the population is under the government's official poverty line;[15] the death rate is 70 percent higher than in urban areas; and the level of social services ranges from abysmal to nonexistent. One survey reported that 75 percent of rural births are attended only by untrained medical practitioners.[16] The Center for Science and the Environment has found that 98 percent of India's rural population do not have toilets and 70 percent are without access to a safe water supply.[17]

The *Wall Street Journal* claims that India's problems can be solved as quickly as it "imports the benefits of the West's industrial revolution and market economics." But those "market economics," imported as part and parcel of the Green Revolution, have meant that Indian food production is increasingly divorced from feeding the Indian masses. For instance, the high-yielding varieties of grains stressed under the Green Revolution produce more cash, but they are also higher in carbohydrates and poorer in protein than traditional crops such as pulses,* groundnuts, peas and beans — which have been relatively ignored according to the dictates of market economics. The result is that while total production of cereal, a favored crop of the Green Revolution, has increased since 1956, per capita consumption of pulses — the "poor man's protein" — declined from 70 grams in 1956 to 39 grams in 1982. According to government estimates, 30,000 children go blind every year due to Vitamin A deficiency, and studies by the National Institute of Nutrition in Hyderabad reveal that 63 percent of India's children up to three years old suffer from iron-deficiency anemia.[18]

Warren Anderson stated that pesticides save 10 percent of India's annual foodcrop, "enough to feed over 70 million people." Pesticides may save food, but that certainly doesn't mean that it is used to feed the Indian masses.† The emphasis on market economics has produced enough food to feed the growing upper and middle classes in urban areas, while the majority of Indians remain malnourished. In fact, the National Sample Survey reported that the daily per capita calorie intake in the country as a

---

*The edible seeds of peas, beans, and lentils, and similar plants having pods.

†Nor, for that matter, does it mean that the pesticides or other modern inputs will even be used on food crops. The pesticides produced at Union Carbide's Bhopal plant were used mainly on cotton, not food. (UCIL boasts that its Sevin pesticide serves "cotton, paddy, and other cash crop farmers most effectively.")[21]

whole declined between 1961–62 and 1971–72. Diets in nearly half the households surveyed in different states of the country were deficient. And a recent survey of nineteen villages located in eight states found that almost one half of the population is unable to satisfy its hunger all year round, with more than a third remaining hungry for three months or more.[19]

According to the National Nutrition Bureau, this means that, "Of the 23 million infants born in the country every year, only 3 million may be truly healthy. Of the rest, 7 million are likely to suffer from minor forms of malnutrition. Three million are expected to die before they reach childhood. And 9 million would enter adulthood with impaired physical stamina and reduced mental ability because of severe malnutrition. Thus, only 15 percent of the children would have full genetic potential of growth and physical and mental development."[20]

The growth of the capitalist mode of agriculture in some regions and sections of India has also produced the spectacle of exporting "surplus" food, often to already relatively well-fed, industrialized countries, while much of India's own population goes hungry. The authors of *Food First* note that "India exports such excellent staples as potatoes to countries like Sweden and the Soviet Union yet the amount of potatoes available to the Indian people has been reduced by 12 percent between 1972 and 1974."[22] It is also estimated that in the Third World, between 50 and 70 percent of pesticides are used on export crops destined for Europe, Japan, and the U.S.[23]

In India and other Third World countries, such food exports are considered vitally necessary to meet the country's foreign exchange requirements and foreign debt payments – debts run up and foreign exchange required, in part, to pay for and continue to import the modern agricultural inputs demanded by Green Revolution-type programs. As the example of India demonstrates, such a policy has proven to be a treadmill to continued poverty and increased dependence, not the path to growth and rising living standards for the vast majority of the people.

UCIL provides a clear example of this "food for export" phenomenon. Between 1971 and 1983, the subsidiary operated a fleet of modern fishing trawlers to catch and process shrimp, off the southwest and southeast coasts of India. The catch was entirely exported to the U.S. and Japan, amid complaints that such mass production methods were depleting traditional fishing grounds upon which many in the southern state of Kerala depended for food and livelihood. The entire program was supported by the Indian government on the basis that it increased India's foreign exchange earnings. UCIL's shrimp operation was only discontinued in 1983 because of "unfavorable market conditions."[24]

What about the bottom-line claim for the Green Revolution — that despite dislocations and unevenness, it has at least improved agricultural efficiency? Even this is only partially true. While overall agricultural production has grown, output in vast areas of India and in certain crops has not. The rate of growth of agricultural production is slowing down and productivity is falling. While all the inputs put together increased at the rate of 3.9 percent per year between 1970–71 and 1983–84, agricultural productivity — output per input applied — fell by 16 percent. Productivity has even declined in crops favored by the Green Revolution such as rice. The Center for Monitoring the Indian Economy declared, "We have been witnessing. . . the revolution in inputs *without a corresponding revolution in output.* "[25]

These agrarian problems are attributable in part to the Green Revolution. For instance, the emphasis on profitable production has meant that dryland farming and traditional crops have been ignored in favor of profitable cash crops. Yet roughly 70 percent of India's cultivated land is not irrigated,[26] and 70 percent of the country's population depends upon it and traditional crops for sustenance.[27] Whole regions of the country, whose climate and terrain were not considered favorable enough for intensive investment, have also been ignored. Today, two-thirds of the rice procured for the market comes from just two states, Punjab and Haryana, and 98 percent of its wheat from three — these two plus Uttar Pradesh. Punjab's agricultural productivity is double the rest of the country's, the amount of land irrigated there is nearly triple. And because of these advantages, Punjab continues to receive a disproportionate share of research and development funds. For instance, Punjab's allocation for crop husbandry and research is nearly four times that of states with triple the population.[28]

Obviously, ignoring the vast bulk of the farming population and most regions in the country has done little to make full use of the country's potential or increase overall agricultural output. It also heightens the distorted character of India's agrarian sector and economy overall. For example, concentrating food supplies in a relatively few areas increases transportation costs, the chance of spoilage in transit, and the chance of marketing bottlenecks. And it further divorces the masses from food supplies in backward states, where National Sample Survey statistics show the nutritional situation is "going from bad to worse."[29]

The particular methods promoted in the Green Revolution are responsible for production problems as well. Extensive use of fertilizers and pesticides, along with ending crop mixing and rotation in favor of heavy, if not exclusive, reliance on HYVs (and planting of cash crops), has led to the poisoning and exhaustion of the soil, putting farmers on the treadmill of ever-increasing use of chemical inputs, and contributing to declining rates of agricultural productivity. The *Times of India* reported that in the state of Gujarat, cotton farmers sprayed their fields six to eight times annually ten years ago. Today they spray anywhere from 20 to 30 times annually, with pesticides accounting for 50 to 60 percent of the cost of cultivation.[30]

Heavy use of pesticides can have other harmful side effects. Most HYVs are less naturally resistant to pests than local varieties, necessitating intense pesticide use. Pesticides kill pests, but also kill their predators. This, combined with the fact that many pests develop resistance to insecticides, creates new and more deadly cycles of pest infestation and lost output – necessitating more and more pesticide use.

The methods promoted by the Green Revolution have also actually helped worsen the terrible health situation in India, beyond the direct poisoning of thousands by pesticides. For instance, the over-reliance on pesticides in both agriculture and the public health field has led to the evolution of new, pesticide-resistant, disease-spreading strains of insects. India's Center for Science and the Environment notes that overuse of pesticides is particularly pronounced in cotton growing operations – the main crop Carbide's Sevin is used for. As a result, mosquitoes which spread diseases such as malaria, filariasis, kala-azar, and

Japanese encephalitis can no longer be controlled by DDT. After having declined from some 100 million cases in 1952 to about 100 thousand in 1965, reported cases of malaria once again shot up to 6.4 million by 1976, and the total remains about 2 million per year today.[31]

The Green Revolution and other imperialist-sponsored development programs have also been advertised as programs for agricultural self-sufficiency. Their effect has been exactly the opposite, engendering new forms of dependence on international capital.

This whole "revolution" depends upon inputs such as fertilizers, pesticides, and farm machinery. Most of these inputs, however, are available only from multinational concerns. For example, some five companies control 50 percent of the world's pesticide production.[32] Of the thirty companies making technical grade (high strength) pesticides in India today, half have either foreign technical collaboration agreements or equity participation with foreign firms, including such giants as Bayer, American Cyanamid, Stauffer Chemical, Rohm and Haas, Monsanto, Ciba-Geigy, and Royal Dutch Shell, as well as Union Carbide.[33] In 1979, over 69 percent of the units in the agricultural machinery industry in India had foreign collaboration. India's fertilizer industry has also been heavily penetrated by foreign capital.[34]

The Green Revolution has also strengthened the bonds of dependence in less direct, but equally significant ways. The continued impoverishment of the Indian countryside has limited the growth of the country's internal market, forcing India to turn outward for markets for its goods, including, ironically, food. Increased dependence on agricultural inputs from the industrial nations is one reason why, in the 1970s, Indian imports grew much more rapidly than exports, leaving the country with a trade deficit of $4.6 billion in 1983–84.[35] Despite all the hoopla surrounding the Green Revolution, India has had to depend upon imported food in all but four years since 1965.[36]

Thus the Green Revolution illustrates the fact that the import or "transfer" of Western technology to the Third World doesn't represent some sort of neutral progress and development, or modernization in the abstract. Just as Union Carbide exports pesticide technology to India based upon its own global interests rather than the lives and safety of the Indian people, so too has the Green Revolution as a whole been shaped to the interests of imperialism. This technological "revolution" was not essentially about feeding the world's hungry, but rather, as Susan George puts it in *How the Other Half Dies*, a "complex system for foreign agribusiness domination of how, where and what Third World farms will produce and at what cost."[37]

Such "revolutions" are part of and contribute to the lopsided development of the world – in which the Third World, containing 75 percent of the world's population, accounts for only 21 percent of total Gross National Product; where five hundred million people go hungry and forty million die of hunger and malnutrition each year, while food resources – even of the countries facing famine and starvation – are channeled into production for the industrialized metropoles.[38] It is part of a system of global relations in which in 1973, 36 out of 40 of the world's poorest countries – those classified by the United Nations as being most seriously affected by inflated world food prices – exported agricultural commodities to the United States.[39] Where half the land in Senegal is devoted to peanut production, largely for the European market, exacerbating the desertification of the country while starvation plagues large parts of Africa. Where vast stretches of jungle in Central America have been cleared for beef production, in large part to feed the voracious appetite of the U.S. fast food industry, while the average Central American consumes less beef than a typical pet cat in the U.S.[40]

This is the reality behind the *Wall Street Journal*'s claim that the use of modern agricultural technology in India has brought "a better life to millions of rural people," and Warren Anderson's argument that "without the technologies and the capital that multinationals help to introduce, developing countries would have little hope of eradicating poverty and hunger." In fact, these "technologies and capital" – or more accurately, the relations of economic and political domination that they reflect and engender – contribute to the continuation and actual intensification of Third World poverty and hunger.

6 | India's Complicity and Dependence

Union Carbide Corporation's summation of the Bhopal disaster hinges in large part on its contention that its Indian subsidiary, UCIL, was acting independently of and without the knowledge of headquarters, ignoring company policies and procedures. As has been demonstrated in previous chapters, this argument is groundless because it ignores UCC's global organization and control of its subsidiaries, and the fundamental and almost total dependence of these subsidiaries on UCC. It also ignores the fact that UCC itself was responsible for and therefore certainly knew about the various maintenance and other cost cutbacks which led to the many procedural violations and played a major role in what transpired on December 2–3.

This contention of a subsidiary "out of control" is paralleled by the now prominent argument that nationalist inspired over-regulation of foreign capital by the Indian government also worked to remove effective control of UCIL from UCC's hands and was a fundamental cause of the disaster. These regulations supposedly prevented or discouraged Union Carbide from operating its Bhopal factory according to the "high standards" followed in the U.S., instead mandating that the design and running of the factory be left in the hands of technologically unsophisticated Indians.

This thesis has been promulgated in *Business Week*, given prominent play in the *New York Times*, and is a key element in Union Carbide's July 31, 1985 affidavit to dismiss the suits filed against it in U.S. courts.[1] One of the strongest versions of this argument appeared in a January 26, 1985 column in the *Wall Street Journal*: "Restrictive Indian foreign-investment regulations that mandate significant local participation and sourcing, along-side economic self-sufficiency policies, may have reduced Union Carbide's motivation and/or capacity to ensure adequate environmental and industrial safety at its Bhopal plant, largely by diluting the degree of parent control," the authors contend. "Indeed regulations driven by nationalism may lie at the core of any in-depth explanation of Bhopal's tragedy.... When control over an affiliate is diluted, and rewards from the activities of that affiliate are depressed, fewer resources are typically committed by the parent."[2]

This is simply cold-blooded blackmail. A major U.S. multinational has just caused the death of thousands and the injury of tens of thousands more. Ignoring safety in order to extract maximum returns was a fundamental cause of the slaughter. Now apologists of the corporation (and Western capital generally) demand more "rewards" for its "activities" and *less* regulation and other concessions, as a price for their investments.

Not only is this arrogant in the extreme, but it twists inside out the actual relationship between the Indian government and foreign capital. In fact there is little real regulation of Union Carbide or foreign capital in general in India – environmental regulation certainly included. Nor is this glaring lack of regulation a matter of mere corruption or bureaucratic incompetence, although there is plenty of both, but flows from and reflects India's basic dependence on and subservience to foreign capital.

India, like the other countries of the Third World, has been locked into a structure of dependence that is manifested in a general acquiescence to the demands of foreign capital, seen as necessary to continue on its charted path of development, and in this particular case in the complicity of the Indian government in helping Union Carbide obscure and cover over the causes and

dimensions of the Bhopal disaster. It has been the object of imperial appetites and conquest since the Portuguese captured the
port city of Goa and set up the first colonial trading outpost in
1510. By 1818 the British had conquered most of what is now
India and ruled it outright until independence in 1947. India's
vast market, strategic geographic location, plentiful resources,
and one of the world's largest pools of cheap labor earned it the
title of "crown jewel" of the British empire.

Since independence, India has sought to overcome its economic backwardness and impoverishment by pursuing a path of
industrial modernization heavily weighted toward importing
industry and technology from the highly industrialized countries.
It has encouraged billions in direct foreign investment and since
1948, 8,407 foreign collaboration agreements have been approved in the private sector.[3] It has secured billions in loans and
aid and negotiated various trade- and technology-sharing agreements with the industrialized powers. These deals have been made
with both the Eastern and Western blocs, in both the private and
the public sectors.

India's size and strategic importance have allowed it some
freedom to maneuver in the cracks created by global rivalries,
particularly between East and West, and gain some economic
leverage. For example, when, during much of the 1950s and
1960s Western capital refused to assist India in developing its
public sector, in particular the capital goods and arms industries,
the Soviet Union was willing to do so, largely to gain greater influence in India. On the other hand, India has tried to take advantage of the U.S.'s desire to keep it out of the Soviet orbit, which
was one motivation for U.S. sponsorship of the "Green Revolution," and to increase capital investment today – which India
greatly desires.

Politically, Indian officials describe this as "nonalignment." In
reality it means that both superpower blocs have their claws deep
into India, which remains dependent in particular ways on each.
Indeed, there are technologically advanced sectors in the Indian
economy – the nuclear power industry being one example. And
India does make a practice of trying to obtain full production
facilities, rather than simply assembly plants. But these have
brought neither all-round, articulated development nor economic

independence. Rather, the pattern of technological dependence spawned by foreign capital, discussed in earlier chapters around Union Carbide's Bhopal operation and also the "Green Revolution," repeats itself throughout the Indian economy, in regard to the aid, loans, and investments by both the Soviet and the Western camps.

For instance, assistance is often double-tied: agreements generally stipulate what type of project the aid is to be used for, and also that needed goods and technology for that project must be purchased from the lending country. Thus the type of project encouraged generally fits into the global needs of the donor — which imports it needs, which goods it can produce more profitably abroad, or what production it wants encouraged in the Third World.

Such stipulations, and the nature of the technology imported, also mean that foreign-assisted industrial projects generally depend on a continued inflow of materials, equipment, or technological assistance from the donor country, creating a whole new surge of costly imports and new forms of dependence. For example, the Soviet Union has set up aircraft plants in India that manufacture MIG fighters, seemingly a breakthrough since imperialist countries don't generally allow advanced military hardware to be produced in the Third World. MIGs are now the backbone of the Indian air force, but the Soviets maintain complete control of the project since complex parts are still imported, and it won't share the basic designs with India. One study noted that if the Soviets pulled out, "India would not be in a position to undertake the manufacture of any other aircraft in these factories."[4] And the Indian air force must obtain the newer, more advanced versions of the MIG directly from the Soviet Union.

The pattern is similar for aid and loans from the West. The World Bank has supplied 40 percent of India's post-independence economic assistance,[5] and has used its leverage to insist on giving key projects to Western companies, even when Indian companies were technologically capable, and on opening up Indian markets to foreign capital. In the 1960s, the World Bank forced the Indian government to permit Western fertilizer firms to price their own products and distribute them in India, as well as set up joint ventures inside the country. According to Susan George, "American businessmen insisted on importing all the necessary machines and equipment for fertilizer plants under construction, even though India could have provided some of them. They also insisted on importing liquid ammonia, instead of using plentiful, Indian-produced naptha as the fertilizer feedstock. Finally, they were able to fix the prices, the distribution circuits and the profit margin."[6]

In the 1960s, the World Bank also used its leverage to assume a greater role in India's overall economic policy, including a critical role in assessing Indian economic plans, in judging their performance under the economic plans, and in determining the amount of aid that should be supplied by consortium members. The Bank was also able to enforce a rupee devaluation and lowering of import restrictions.[7]

India's strategy has been to pay for such foreign assistance and projects through boosting exports; in fact, many foreign-sponsored projects are developed specifically to produce for export. But generally the technology exported to India has not helped it to compete effectively on the world market. Such projects are relatively inefficient and uncompetitive because the technology involved is generally not first-rate, and/or the projects remain dependent upon imports and assistance from the donor country and are not supported by a well-developed and articulated economic base in India. India continues to rely heavily on traditional raw material exports, whose prices fluctuate wildly on the world market, and bring India little trading leverage.[8]

Over 60 percent of India's exports go to and 40 percent of its imports come from the industrialized nations, with the Soviet Union and the U.S. ranking one and two among India's trading partners.[9] Yet the terms of this trade are often dictated by imperialism as repayment for loans and technology, at what amount to extortionist rates. India lost an estimated 80 million rupees per year during the 1960s because it was paid less than world market prices for tea exported to the USSR. Goods exported to the Soviet Union from India are often "switched," i.e., resold to other countries at higher prices. For instance, in the late 1960s, Indian pig iron purchased at 30.5 rubles per ton was resold in Africa at 169 rubles per ton. Indian cashews traded to the Soviets were ending up in the U.S., shoes in Belgium, and tea in Western Europe.[10]

This path of development represents a downward spiral of debt and dependence. The rate of yearly industrial growth declined from 7.6 percent annually between 1950–51 and 1965–66 to 4.5 percent from 1965–66 to 1983–84.[11] In the 1970s, Indian imports grew three times as fast as in the previous decade, soon outstripping exports by 60 percent. Meanwhile, India's share of world exports fell from 2.2 percent in 1948–49 to 0.5 percent in 1982–83, leaving it with a trade deficit of $4.6 billion in 1983–84.[12]

This trade deficit means that India is unable to pay its mounting debts for imports and loans for technology — and is forced to turn again to loans and foreign capital for more and more assistance. The Indian government owes world financial institutions $18.5 billion. In 1983 its account surplus couldn't cover the $790 million in interest it owed on its foreign debt. "These debt service payments are managed only by further borrowing! . . . We are the foremost beggar in the world," writes the Center for Monitoring the Indian Economy (CMIE) in Bombay. Since 1961, India has also received some $26.5 billion in foreign assistance, nearly 40 percent coming from the World Bank. "We have become addicts to foreign economic assistance," adds the CMIE.[13] Since 1970, Indian loan repayments to the Soviet Union have exceeded the amount of foreign aid received. In 1978–79, for instance, India received 139 million rupees from the USSR but had to pay back 567 million.[14]

In addition to aid and loans, India has also been forced into greater reliance on direct foreign investment. In an article entitled "Red Carpet for Foreign Capital," *Economic & Political Weekly* of Bombay notes that there was a big wave of foreign collaboration between 1956 and 1965, ostensibly aimed at increasing India's self-reliance through import substitution and technology "transfer."* Yet this surge in foreign collaborations only paved the way for an even bigger wave of foreign investment from the middle '70s to the present. A record 730 foreign collaboration

---

*According to the *Times of India*, Union Carbide described the MIC production plant in Bhopal as an "import-substitution" project that would save India some $3.8 million per year in foreign exchange that had previously been spent to import MIC for the Bhopal plant.[16]

agreements were signed in 1984, up from the previous record of 591 set the year before and 271 in 1975. Among the reasons cited by the magazine for the surge in agreements were declining foreign aid, the pressure of unchecked elitist consumption demand, and production for export to meet India's rapidly increasing foreign debts and trade deficit.[15]

One of the most revealing – and outrageous – illustrations of the dependence of Third World countries like India upon foreign capital was provided by a *New York Times* article. Noting that many Third World countries, cash-starved and deeply in debt, look to foreign direct investment as their only source of capital and technology, it then comments, "Not even the chemical disaster at the Union Carbide Corporation plant in Bhopal, India, seems to have made countries noticeably more nervous about foreign investment."[17]

Partly to assuage nationalist sentiment, partly to mitigate against the abuses mentioned above, India does regulate foreign investment to an extent. It specifies which sectors of the economy are open to foreign capital, directing it into certain "core" sectors such as shipbuilding, metallurgy, chemicals and pesticides, industrial instruments, electrical and electronic supplies, and pharmaceuticals – generally high-tech industries. Foreign exchange transactions and the amount of equity that can be held by foreign corporations are also controlled. There are government regulations concerning the import of capital goods and materials, and the hiring of foreign technicians, which stress that wherever possible Indian goods and labor should be employed.

While these regulations are ostensibly designed to give India self-sufficiency and control of the Indian economy, they neither represent hostility to foreign investment nor help to achieve independence or even fundamental control of foreign capital. In fact, these regulations are themselves shaped by the needs of imperialism and India's dependence on foreign capital and technology. For example, foreign investment is "directed" into high-tech sectors of the economy. But these are precisely the areas in which foreign capital enjoys the greatest competitive advantage and would be most likely to invest in any event, and where India, on the other hand, is most dependent.

Under the 1973 Foreign Exchange Regulations Act (FERA),

foreign capital is limited to 40 percent ownership of Indian subsidiaries. But foreign corporations can be granted exemptions from these regulations if they employ advanced technology and contribute to foreign-exchange earnings. (Union Carbide was granted a majority 50.9 percent ownership of UCIL because it met these stipulations.) Even in situations where a foreign concern is a "minority" owner in a venture, its control of technological inputs, trademarks, marketing, and sources of capital may give it effective control. (Such factors also make it quite possible to control any corporation with less than 50 percent of the stock.)*

Multinational companies are required to hire and train Indians and to use indigenous materials and equipment whenever possible. But this is quite compatible with the interests and mode of operation of foreign capital, which often locates in the Third World, in part, to take advantage of cheaper labor and materials. For instance, Indian managers and technicians, not to mention unskilled workers, earn a pittance of what similarly skilled employees do in the U.S. (The head of Union Carbide's research and development lab, a Ph.D., trained in the U.S., with 26 years of experience, earns around $6,000 a year in salary — half that of an entry-level production worker in the U.S.).[19]

It also must be noted that these are general guidelines, subject to the needs of promoting industry and commerce, not hard and fast rules. UCIL didn't have an Indian managing director for nearly fifty years, until 1977. The Bhopal plant was run by an American until 1982, and when the MIC unit was built, Carbide brought technicians from West Virginia to teach Indians to run

---

*In order to bolster its claim that Indian government regulations effectively place UCIL in Indian hands, Union Carbide makes the point in its July 31, 1985 affidavit that 49.1 percent of UCIL stock is owned by "Indian citizens and business entities," and that a "substantial amount" is owned by "entities controlled by the Indian Government." It also makes the point that, "At no time did Union Carbide participate in the financing of the Bhopal plant, nor did it directly or indirectly guarantee any loans extended to UCIL."[18] But this merely illustrates the advantages of joint ventures for foreign capital. Union Carbide not only did not have to provide all the financing for its own Indian operation, even though it retained control and received the bulk of the profits from it, but joint ownership also provided the corporation with powerful and influential connections in the Indian government and business community.

the process. Initially they were to stay there for one year, but "extensions were granted."[20]

The January 26 *Wall Street Journal* article complains that multinationals aren't offered sufficient "rewards" in countries like India, partly because of regulations that mandate Indian equity participation. Yet one 1980 study by the Indo-U.S. Chamber of Commerce found that between 1973–74 and 1978–79, foreign subsidiaries (which often have Indian participation) averaged a 15 percent rate of return on their assets, and over 24 percent in the pharmaceuticals and motor vehicles industries. These rates were two to three times higher than rates of returns for large Indian companies, and, ironically, branches of foreign companies – wholly owned by the parent – as well.[21] Furthermore, India places few restrictions on the repatriation of profits.

Most multinationals also recognize the value of "nationalist" regulations such as India's in providing a favorable political climate for their operations – and their host government – without compromising their control of the essentials. Kenneth Rush, a former Union Carbide vice president and undersecretary of state, said, "It's absolutely essential to have that kind of approach [indigenization]. It allows you to greatly lessen such political pressures as drives for nationalization. It also helps you to attract the best talent from the country."[22]

S. Kumaraswami, in charge of Union Carbide's relations with the Indian government, made it clear that the company's relationship with the Indian government was a friendly one, based on a mutual desire to promote industrialization, and characterized by "flexibility and understanding." He stressed that government regulations were no big impediment to running the company as Carbide saw fit.[23]

Union Carbide states, "The Indian Government controlled to a large extent the sources of material and equipment used in the construction and operation of the Bhopal plant."[24] While licenses were required for capital goods and process materials imports, according to Union Carbide's own Kumaraswami they were easy to obtain if the needed equipment was not available in India. In Bhopal there were "20 or 30 pages" of items imported for the MIC production unit, worth some 1.8 crore rupees (approximately $1.4 million). This is an indication that any lack of state-of-the-art equipment – including safety equipment – at the Bhopal plant wasn't the result of overly strict Indian government regulations – if the equipment was needed, it could be imported. In 1982 and 1983, over 30 percent of the raw materials, spare parts, and components used by UCIL as a whole were imported, again demonstrating that import restrictions were not overly stringent.[25]

If anything, these already-toothless regulations are becoming even weaker under the pressure of India's economic difficulties. India's financial daily, *Business Standard*, describes the import policy for 1982-83 as the most liberal since independence. It also commented that the easing of import restrictions on some industrial machinery, equipment, raw materials and components, has led to dumping of foreign goods and serious harm to indigenous industry.[26]

Not only is the domination by and dependence on foreign capital one of the key factors shaping India's overall regulations; it affects environmental and safety regulations as well, and is central to understanding why many of these were not applied to Union Carbide's plant in Bhopal.

India has a number of environmental and safety laws on the books that are directly relevant to Union Carbide's Bhopal plant. Industrial licenses are issued by the central government's Ministry of Industry, in consultation with other relevant federal bodies. However, the overwhelming emphasis at the federal level is economic; the capital and foreign exchange requirements, power and transport needs, the needs of the Indian market, etc., are the primary factors considered in licensing new industry, including industry with foreign participation. Questions of safety and environmental impact are relegated to the state governments, which is itself an indication of how important they are considered by the Indian government. A number of more specific federal environmental laws have only recently been enacted,[27] and India's federal environmental department, itself a new creation, has a staff of only 150 for the whole country.[28]

In 1970, UCIL first proposed expanding the plant to include the capacity to manufacture MIC-based pesticides from scratch. In 1973, Carbide reached an agreement in principle with the

Indian government to undertake the expansion and was issued an industrial license in 1975. Securing approval involved a number of government agencies, at both the federal and state levels. At no time were serious questions about the dangers of MIC production raised. In fact, when Union Carbide first applied for a Ministry of Industry license, the application made no mention of the environmental impact at all.[29]

At the state level, Union Carbide applied to Bhopal's Town and Country Planning Directorate in 1972 for permission to expand its site on the northern edge of Bhopal from 5 to 55 acres to accommodate the planned production plant. According to the *Hindustan Times*, this application clearly showed buildings labeled "MIC production unit" and "MIC storage tanks."[30] But the Indian press reports that rather than this provoking intensive questioning, "Those familiar with the circumstances in which the MIC-based pesticides unit was set up indicated that there was minimum procedural delay on the part of the authorities in meeting the Union Carbide requirements," and that the UCIL proposal was approved within one year.[31]

When this expansion was approved, neither water nor air pollution laws were on the books. The Bhopal town plan regulating land usage was still in its formative stages, and nationally there were no regulations concerning the locating of hazardous industries.*

But the problem in Bhopal wasn't simply a lack of environmental legislation. Even the laws that were on the books were ignored in the case of Union Carbide. In August 1975, two months before Union Carbide's license to produce MIC was approved and five years before production actually began, the Bhopal Town and Country Planning Act came into force. This plan earmarked 150 hectares on the northeast side of the city — well away and downwind from populated areas — for "obnoxious and hazardous" industries. "Insecticides, Fungicides and Pesticides" were on the list of hazardous and obnoxious industries.

---

*Regulations concerning the locating of industry near populous areas and stipulating that environmental clearances be issued before industrial licenses are granted have only been enacted in the past couple of years. Their effectiveness remains open to question.[32]

The plan specifically lists a number of factories that have to be relocated to the obnoxious zone. Sixteen concerns, including a glue factory, a sawmill, a slaughter house, and a tannery were listed as "incompatible" and ordered relocated. Union Carbide, the main pesticide producer in the area, wasn't mentioned.[33]

Officials in Bhopal today offer two main reasons for this decision. One, that the Bhopal plant was located before the town plan came into effect, making its relocation difficult. This is obviously hollow since the sixteen industries ordered relocated under the town plan were also in existence. The other reason given was that the plant was relatively emission free.

But the bottom line was the Madhya Pradesh government's need to attract and accommodate large industry, a need which led them to offer Union Carbide such generous concessions in the first place. Madhya Pradesh is one of India's poorest and least developed states, with a per capita income 30 percent lower than India as a whole, and roughly half the level of industrialization.[34] "Union Carbide is a very large and well-known chemical firm with international ramifications, which would be very attractive to a state with low employment like Madhya Pradesh," commented M. N. Buch, author of the planning act and formerly principal secretary to the government of Madhya Pradesh, commissioner and director of town and country planning, and secretary of environment and administrator of the Bhopal municipal corporation. "The general idea was once you get a Union Carbide or Monsanto or whatever, then you can use this as a lever to attract more industry to the state."[35]

The same Bhopal Town and Country Planning Act that sets aside an area for hazardous industry speaks glowingly of Carbide as one of the industries that have made Bhopal "a nerve-centre of Regional Trade and Commerce-cum-Industrial centre," and notes that the Union Carbide Research and Development facility was among the institutions that "lends Bhopal a status of educational-cum-research centre of national and State importance."[36] Buch said he proposed relocating the Carbide plant in 1975 to conform with the Planning Act, but was opposed by Union Carbide and others in the Madhya Pradesh administration.

If there was little scrutiny of Carbide's Bhopal pesticide production unit during the planning stages, things didn't improve once the operation got underway. The Madhya Pradesh Department of Labor is charged with regulating industry and ensuring worker safety. But the responsibilities are defined in an extremely narrow way, dealing mainly with things like ventilation, dust, fencing of machinery, latrines, and drinking water. Fines for violating safety regulations are so low that "managements smilingly pay them and go back and commit the same offense," according to one chief inspector.[37]

Further, the enforcement machinery is extremely limited. In Madhya Pradesh, each factory inspector is responsible for between 150 and 286 factories — depending on whose figures one accepts — with a quota of 400 inspections in 200 working days, far more than inspectors can handle. Most regulatory departments have few instruments, primitive equipment, and few if any cars to transport inspectors to factories. One inspector reported having to travel to the factories he was to inspect in the cars of the factory management.[38] The Bhopal pollution control board doesn't even have adequate equipment to monitor emissions.[39]

India's technological backwardness and dependence further limits its regulation of industry, particularly foreign-owned, high-tech industries. Regulatory agencies in Bhopal, for instance, didn't have the equipment needed to monitor a plant like Carbide's. The *New York Times* reports that inspectors did check Carbide's MIC tanks, but relied on "ultrasonic tests performed by the company itself."[40] After the disaster, Indian government officials had to use Carbide equipment to test the remaining MIC, both to determine how to neutralize it and what had caused the disaster.[41]

The technological gap between a company like Carbide and most of the agencies mandated to regulate it is also widened by the awe in which some of India's regulators and government officials hold modern corporations like Union Carbide. "Because of Union Carbide's reputation as one of the top companies in the world, the factory inspectorate used to rely on their safety systems," commented Ravi Shevade, a chemical engineer and environmental activist from Bombay who studied the Bhopal plant after the disaster. "It was a kind of psychological dependence: they're bound to be state-of-the-art systems and what do we know?"[42]

Given all this, it isn't surprising that inspections of the Carbide plant were generally perfunctory and petty, never raising questions about the plant's basic operation and design. These were considered unchangeable givens, and enforcement of safety standards was left essentially in Union Carbide's hands.[43]

This routine didn't change even when serious accidents raised troubling questions about the plant. After the October 6, 1982 leak of MIC and other gases sent three workers to the hospital and affected 15 more, an inspector visited the plant. His report blamed the accident on failure to follow company procedures. No questions were asked about why workers didn't have gas masks. The fact that people in the surrounding neighborhoods were affected by the gas wasn't mentioned in the report, nor were questions raised about the need for informing the community of the potential dangers of MIC and developing an evacuation plan.

But probably the most blatant case of regulatory irresponsibility followed the death of the one worker, Ashraf Khan, from phosgene poisoning in 1981. The inspector visited the factory on December 26, two days after the accident, and three more times in the ensuing week. His "detailed inquiry" ended up blaming Ashraf Khan for his own death: "accident occurred due to the deceased inhaling phosgene after removing the breathing mask." No mention was made of the fact that phosgene should never have been in the pipeline in the first place when the MIC unit isn't working, since it is supposed to be utilized immediately and not stored. Nor were questions raised about why the head of the production department hadn't certified that the pipeline had been cleared of phosgene, before the maintenance began, as plant regulations stipulate. Instead, the inspector recommended that workers be more careful when opening such pipelines.*[44]

It wasn't as if the local authorities hadn't been warned of all the dangers. As already indicated, the Workmen's Union had

---

*The Madhya Pradesh Department of Labor did, however, commission a more in-depth investigation of the incident by a professor at a nearby science college. His report, which raised some sharp concerns about the fundamental safety of the plant, was delivered to the Department on March 4, 1984, over two years after the accident. Seven months later, when gas enveloped Bhopal, the report was still gathering dust in the Department of Labor.[45]

been complaining of unsafe conditions since the mid-'70s. More alarms were sounded following the death of Ashraf Khan. One local journalist undertook an investigation of the plant after Ashraf Khan died. The headlines in the September and October 1982 issues of his weekly *Rapat* – which he mailed to all the responsible officials – summed up his conclusions: "Bhopal Sitting on the Brink of a Volcano," "Sage, Please Save This City," and "If You Don't Understand, All Will Perish."[46]

The Indian authorities responded to these warnings with a debate in the Madhya Pradesh legislature on December 21, 1982. The state labor minister spelled out the government's priorities immediately: "Mr. Speaker, this plant was established here in 1969 with an investment of 25 crore rupees. It is not a small piece of stone that I can shift from one place to another. This factory has nationwide links." He then assured the legislators that he had visited the factory three times, and "there is no danger to the city, nor do I find any symptoms of it."

When pushed for proof, he insisted that Union Carbide's safety precautions precluded any danger. "Safety measures have been taken at the factory with full responsibility. In the event of a gas leak, the siren would immediately blow and the water sprayers situated all around begin functioning at full speed." Asked about the dangers of the gases used at the plant, he responded, "There is no report that suggests that the poisonous gas has any adverse affect on the workers."[47]

Bhopal is typical of the safety and environmental regulatory situation throughout India. The *Hindustan Times* reports that "Only 16 out of the 50 pesticide manufacturing units in the country have any worthwhile pollution control system working and the general system of supervision of pollution control is dangerously lax."[48] A 1981 survey by the Central Board for Prevention and Control of Water Pollution found that of 1,700 large and medium-sized industries polluting water, only 460 had effluent treatment facilities.[49] And few factories have ever set up legislatively mandated safety committees.[50]

The net result of these lax environmental and safety regulations has been a grim human and ecological toll. The *State of the*

Environment report, published by the Center for Science and the Environment in New Delhi, indicates that 70 percent of all available water in India is polluted, and that levels of air pollution are going up; for example, 60 percent of Calcutta's residents suffer from respiratory ailments because of air pollution.[51]

The Gwalior Rayon Silk Mills, located on the Chambal River in Nagda, Madhya Pradesh, has been responsible for the death of nineteen workers and the spread of crippling diseases among workers and the surrounding population through discharges of carbon disulphide, carbon monoxide, and other pollutants into the air and zinc and mercury into the river. "The entire Nagda town and the surrounding villages within a radius of 5 kms. are a mini gas chamber," wrote one journalist who studied the factory. He estimated its victims at one-half million, 40 percent of whom are children under fourteen.[52]

Industrial accidents have doubled from 30 per thousand workers in 1951 to nearly 67 per thousand in 1980, and fatality rates are "5 to 7 times higher" than those prevailing in Europe and Japan.[53] India's *Industrial Times* reports that "Over the last 30 years, over 3.4 million occupational accidents have been reported. The number of factory accidents and deaths in India has been increasing. In 1975, the total number of accidents was 242,352. It rose to 356,341 in 1980. It jumped to over 500,000 in 1983. The recent statistics released by the Ministry of Labor reveals that no less than 250,000 workers are maimed, crippled or disabled every year."[54]

Some Indian environmentalists argue that the actual toll may be even higher, as factory statistics often don't include industrial diseases and accidents in rural areas are enormously underreported. For instance, a reported one-third of India's asbestos workers suffer from asbestosis.[55] In the Mandsaur district of Madhya Pradesh, more than 2,000 slate workers have died in the past decade due to silicosis. And a 1982 study by India's Department of the Environment found that 25 percent of the workers in battery factories had lead poisoning, 27 percent of rayon workers suffered from overexposure to carbon disulphide, and nearly a third of all workers in DDT plants were ill from its effects.[56]

Some in the U.S. have seized upon India's terrible environmental and safety regulatory record as one more reason to blame

India for the Bhopal disaster; as Union Carbide's July 31 affidavit noted, "At various times before, during and after the construction of the Bhopal plant, the State of Madhya Pradesh certified that the Bhopal plant complied with all of the Indian Environmental Practices and Pollution Abatement Regulations."[57] In other words, Indian authorities failed to make sure the plant was safe. Of course, it is somewhat ironic to hear complaints about Indian "under-regulation," after so much has been made of Indian "over-regulation" of foreign capital.[58] But more to the point, who is fundamentally to blame for this situation? Union Carbide, the *New York Times*, and the *Wall Street Journal* draw a link between over- and under-regulation by complaining that nationalist-inspired over-regulation has put safety decisions in the hands of Third World people who are not only technologically un-sophisticated, but may not be concerned with matters of safety and health. A *New York Times* article following the disaster quotes a U.S. executive, "If you identify what you consider to be a potential hazard in one of these locations, what do you do if local management refuses to act on your recommendations?"[59]

This once again turns things inside out. For example, multi-nationals like Union Carbide routinely export deadly products and processes, often banned in the home country, to the Third World. Following the Bhopal disaster, one U.S. State Department official bluntly told a Congressional subcommittee, "We do not generally apply U.S. environmental and industrial safety laws to activities of multinational enterprises in other countries."[60]

In 1979, the U.S. General Accounting Office reported that fully 25 percent of all pesticides sold overseas by U.S. companies – an estimated 150 million pounds a year – were banned, restricted, or unregistered for use in the U.S.[61] And these deadly chemicals are generally sold without even the minimal labeling, training, or protection for those applying them which is available in the industrialized countries. Union Carbide produces or sells a number of banned or restricted pesticides in the Third World, including DDT, Mirex, Heptachlor, Chlordane, and Endrin.[62]

One result of foreign capital's trade in toxic chemicals is an estimated 375,000 people poisoned and 10,000 killed by pesticides in Third World countries every year. This is one-half of the global total of poisoning and three-quarters of the total of pesticide-related deaths. Yet the Third World accounts for only 15 percent of world pesticide consumption and 30 percent of world insecticide consumption – making Third World death rates from these products ten times as high as those in the industrialized nations. And these figures don't include the long-term, largely unrecorded effects that contact with toxic pesticides has around the world.[63]

The *Times of India* estimates that as much as 70 percent of the pesticides used in India are banned or restricted in the industrialized nations, and that India may account for one-third of all Third World pesticide poisonings.[64] Among Indian women, for example, residues of the pesticides DDT and BHC in breast milk are now 11 and 9.2 times greater, respectively, than in the U.S., where both chemicals are banned.[65]

The pharmaceutical industry provides another example of these dumping practices. U.S. companies sold $8.6 billion worth of drugs overseas in 1979 – many of them banned or highly restricted in the U.S. Yet they are sold over the counter, often without warning labels, in the Third World. The contraceptive Depo-Provera has been linked with cancer and birth defects and is banned in the U.S. But Upjohn and other U.S. corporations still market it in eighty-two countries around the world. In 1969, Albamycin was restricted in the U.S. after it triggered an outbreak of a sometimes fatal blood disease. It continues to be sold in twenty-seven countries. Stockholders of Warner-Lambert provided a sterling example of U.S. capital's *modus operandi*. They voted overwhelmingly against putting the same warning label as used in the U.S. on their potentially dangerous drug, Chloromycetin, when sold overseas.[66]

As for the chemical industry, because of the high rates of cancer resulting from asbestos exposure, production has dropped sharply in the industrialized countries, 60 percent between 1978 and 1982. However, production continues unabated in the underdeveloped countries. At an asbestos plant in Ahmedabad, India, partly owned by Johns-Manville, asbestos dust floats freely throughout the plant, and children living near the plant play in asbestos wastes dumped haphazardly outside. Production of benzidine-based dyes has also been increasingly exported outside of the U.S., including to India, after its carcinogenic properties were discovered.[67] At the Union Carbide battery plant in Jakarta, Indonesia, one investigation found that, "at one point 402 employees, more than half the work force of 750, were suffering from kidney disease attributable to workplace contamination."[68]

A *New York Times* article following the Bhopal disaster complained that excessive Third World government regulation of foreign capital placed advanced technologies in the hands of those who often do not "have what Dr. Utidjian of American Cyanamid calls the 'North American philosophy of the importance of human life.' "[69] This well-worn staple of imperialist mythology, that "life is cheap" in the Third World, has been repeated frequently, in various guises, to explain, and explain away, the disaster in Bhopal. Indeed, life is shorter and filled with more misery in the oppressed countries. Imperialism's domination of them, as reflected in this systematic dumping of deadly hazards, and the disaster in Bhopal, sees to that.

7 | In the Horror's Aftermath

In the aftermath of Bhopal, the main parties involved promised to find out what had caused such a horrible disaster, and declared their determination to prevent such a thing from ever happening again. But their actions stood in sharp contrast to their words. In fact, they proceeded in the very same manner that gave rise to the disaster in the first place.

Warren Anderson, in introducing Union Carbide's March 1985 report, claimed the company had "honored" its promise to "find out what went wrong at Bhopal." Declaring that the lessons of Bhopal "are too important to be based on speculation and conjecture," he turned around and advanced a position based on nothing but speculation and conjecture – the charge of sabotage.[1] The company was raising the specter of terrorism, in an obvious attempt to capitalize on the current political climate in the U.S. and the attacks, verbal and otherwise, against "world terrorism" – and probably to contribute to that climate as well. This was a desperate gambit by Union Carbide designed to obscure its responsibility for the massacre, and sidestep the damaging questions being raised.

At the March 20 press conference, Union Carbide officials were coy about the sabotage charge: "I can't impute malice here and I can't say it's an act of sabotage," stated Anderson. But this was clearly the thrust of the company's position – according to the scenario it constructed, no other explanation was really possible. And, when pushed on the subject by newsmen, Anderson said, "It doesn't seem like something that is inadvertent."[2]

More recently, UCC has become more forthright about its charges. In August 1985, a company spokesman said that it now seemed "more and more likely" that water was deliberately introduced into tank 610.[3] Union Carbide's lawyer stated he is convinced that sabotage was the probable cause of the accident.[4] And the corporation's July 31, 1985 affidavit, after stating the company did not know if the disaster was the result of a deliberate act, raises the question of sabotage several times and goes on to say in so many words exactly that: "A group of Indian Sikh extremists, which calls itself 'Black June,' has claimed responsibility for the incident."[5]

Company officials in India were less circumspect. They directly, albeit privately and off the record, raised the question of sabotage, and linked it to Soviet efforts to destabilize India. The country was going through a highly charged period following the Sikh uprising and suppression, and the assassination of Prime Minister Indira Gandhi that followed, and was moving closer to the West at the same time, the officials said. What better way for the Soviets or some of their surrogates to take advantage of this volatile situation and disrupt this westward drift, they contended, than create an incident involving Union Carbide, the U.S. multinational with the largest direct investments in India?[6]

The substance of Union Carbide's claim is less important than the fact that they made it. The company admits it has absolutely no proof of sabotage. It postulates that the most likely source of water that got into tank 610 was a utility station near the MIC tanks. "The nitrogen and water lines are at the same utility station. If someone had connected a tubing to the water line instead of the nitrogen line either deliberately or intending to introduce nitrogen into the tank, this could account for the presence of water in the tank."[7] But Indian journalists and environmental activists, who have interviewed most of the workers present on the night of December 2, have found no evidence to support the sabotage charge or this particular version of events.[8]

Union Carbide also discounts the possibility that the water washing was responsible for the water contamination because it "would have required simultaneous leaks through several reportedly closed valves, which is highly improbable."[9] But Carbide's "probability" is based not only on ignoring, or covering over, the notoriously poor quality of the valves at the plant, but also the existence of the jumper line connecting the PVH and the RVVH. Of course, at the time of the March 20 report, Union Carbide wasn't admitting the existence of the jumper line.* According to *Sunday* magazine, India's Central Bureau of Investigation, which took control of the plant following the disaster, "disconnected the pipeline from the storage tanks on the morning after the leak, [and] drained out as much as 27 litres of water from the structural on 14 February. This totally refutes the theory of sabotage...being floated by certain company officials. The water was found in almost all connecting pipelines tracing the entire route from the point of washing to the RVVH line" (from where it went through the jumper, into the PVH, and then into tank 610).[10]

The company also argues that after months of "scientific deliberation," it determined that at least 120 to 240 gallons of water would have been necessary to account for the chemistry of the reaction and the residues left over, and such an amount of water could not have flowed through the vent headers into tank 610.[12] First of all, because water washing was going on for nearly three hours before being turned off, it is quite possible that a considerable amount of water did enter the pipelines leading to tank 610. Second, Carbide's chemistry has not been confirmed by independent sources and it has been questioned by, among others, the head of India's Council of Scientific and Industrial Research, Dr. Srinivasan Varadarajan. He argues that only a small amount of water − "between one pint and one quart" − would have been necessary to trigger a chain reaction.†[13]

---

*When Carbide finally admitted the existence of the jumper line, it said that it was a modification, done in India, of the original design. This parallels the company's other efforts to blame the disaster on its Indian subsidiary.[11]

†Dr. Varadarajan argues that a small amount of water, reacting with the phosgene present in tank 610 (phosgene is used to stabilize MIC), could liberate enough heat and chloride ions to trigger a chain reaction.

As for the so-called "Black June" terrorist group, an official at the Indian consulate in New York City said that Carbide reported it had received a call from them claiming credit, and that one such poster to that effect had appeared in Punjab. But other than that, no one had ever heard of the group – it never claimed credit for anything before the disaster, nor has it since – and he dismissed it as a figment of Union Carbide's imagination.[14]

How far Union Carbide goes with its terrorism gambit remains to be seen. But the fact that the corporation raised it at all is quite significant and reveals much about the political currents that it and all the major players in this disaster are swimming in, and the real forces shaping their responses. The disaster in Bhopal took place against the backdrop of severe strains in the fabric of Indian society, and an increasingly tense global contention between the U.S. and Soviet camps, reflected in south Asia by the Soviet invasion of Afghanistan, the U.S. arming of Pakistan, and the heightened competition between the two rivals for influence and position in India itself. Union Carbide's sabotage charge in large part reflects an attempt to put the onus for the disaster on the U.S.'s Soviet rivals and protect U.S. interests in India.

The response of the Soviet Union and its allies to the Bhopal disaster has been shaped by the same sharp superpower rivalry in India and globally. They seized upon the disaster to try and cool the warming trend in relations between the U.S. and India. Articles in the Soviet press, for instance, analyzed the Bhopal catastrophe as the "logical consequence of the general policy pursued by multinational corporations," and listed Bhopal, along with the assassination of Indira Gandhi, and a recent spy scandal in New Delhi, as links "of a single CIA-engineered conspiracy aimed at destabilizing India."[15] The Secretary of the Madhya Pradesh unit of the Soviet-aligned Communist Party of India stated that multinationals were spying for imperialism and shouldn't be allowed into India.[16]

Significantly, pro-Soviet forces focused much of their agitation on the links between the disaster in Bhopal and Western war preparations. The Secretary of the pro-Soviet World Federation of Trade Unions argued that companies like Union Carbide were supplying arms for chemical and biological warfare to NATO countries.[17] Romesh Chandra, President of the pro-Soviet World Peace Council, speaking in Bhopal, claimed that the December 3 gas leak was not an accident but "part of an experiment in chemical warfare" by the U.S. that "went out of control."[18] Charges that Bhopal may have been a "guinea pig" in some chemical warfare experiment, or that Union Carbide was involved — through its R&D facility in Bhopal — in chemical warfare research, were widespread in the Indian press, and vigorously denied by Carbide officials. (Carbide denies having any involvement in chemical or biological warfare research or production at any of its facilities, including in Bhopal.)[19]

It seems unlikely that the gas release was an intentional experiment, or that Carbide's Bhopal R&D facility is directly engaged in chemical warfare research. But such speculation is not at all unreasonable, given the overall world situation, the feverish U.S.-Soviet arms race, and Union Carbide's involvement in other military-related projects. The corporation played a "key role" in the Manhattan project, and, from the late 1940s until 1983, it managed the Department of Energy's Y-12 nuclear plant in Oak Ridge, Tennessee, which produces, among other things, components for nuclear weapons and test devices for weapons design agencies.[20]

India's pro-Soviet organizations did not attempt to launch massive actions following the disaster, or criticize the Indian government's role in Bhopal. These organizations have historically followed a strategy of seeking to gain influence in the ruling Congress-I party. Since the Indian government had a strong interest in calming the situation, large-scale Bhopal-related actions sponsored by these organizations would have disrupted this working relationship and overall strategy.

U.S. officials reacted quickly to contain any possible damage to Indo-U.S. relations arising from Bhopal, and to limit Soviet maneuverings. President Reagan sent a letter to Prime Minister Rajiv Gandhi expressing grief and stating, "Our hearts go out to those who suffer."[21] At Congressional hearings called in December 1984 to "assess the impact of the Bhopal disaster on Indo-American relations," a State Department official said, "From the beginning of the crisis the U.S. government has made clear to Indian authorities our readiness to respond, in a variety of ways, with assistance that the Indian government might identify as useful." The U.S. chargé d'affaires in New Delhi dispatched a disaster relief team to Bhopal to consult with local officials, and a four-person team of experts from the Center for Disease Control in Atlanta was sent to India to aid with the medical relief.[22]

These efforts to control the political damage from the worst industrial disaster in history were coupled with a seemingly calculated disinterest in Bhopal and an arrogant, vigorous defense of the prerogatives of U.S. capital around the globe.

While Reagan declared that his heart went out to the victims, little else did. The U.S. government's Office of U.S. Foreign Disaster Assistance donated $12,400 for the purchase of medical supplies, and the U.S. chargé d'affaires contributed $25,000 to the Indian government's central relief fund.[23] The total amounted to about 19 cents for each person who inhaled Carbide's deadly fumes. No other aid was forthcoming, nor was there any effort to raise funds from among the public. An official at the State Department told why the Administration had been careful not to give much aid: it would have been a "sign of guilt."[24] Less than a week after the Bhopal disaster, President Reagan held a press conference and didn't mention Bhopal a single time (nor did any of the journalists present raise a question about it).[25]

On December 18, 1984, barely two weeks after the Bhopal disaster, the United States cast the lone "no" on a United Nations vote to expand and continue to publish a directory of 500 potentially dangerous products that are banned or restricted in some sixty countries. U.S. officials felt that the $89,000 required to republish the directory was "wasteful," and worried that such a list might create trade barriers.[26] At House Subcommittee on Asian and Pacific Affairs hearings on the disaster, held with little fanfare and even fewer substantive results, the Administration declared it would stick to its policy of not making U.S. corporations follow U.S. environmental guidelines while operating abroad, or even inform the host governments of the hazards of their products or processes.[27] The Congressmen showed no inclination to pursue the issue.

The House Subcommittee on Health and the Environment held lengthier hearings on Bhopal, but from the standpoint of the chemical dangers facing Americans, not those facing Third World peoples as a result of U.S. corporations operating abroad. At these hearings, executives from major U.S. chemical firms, including Warren Anderson, became the latest converts to stricter control of hazardous emissions in the U.S., after years of opposition to such regulations. This was done largely to reestablish public faith in the chemical industry and to head off the possibility of stricter state and local measures. As far as safety practices while operating overseas, these executives promised more voluntary surveillance of these facilities. This was easy enough to say, while there was no mention of any plans or legislation for stricter regulation of U.S. companies operating abroad.[28]

In fact, in the wake of Bhopal, prominent U.S. representatives have made it a point to argue that U.S. capital must not be subject to new environmental regulations or general restrictions while operating in Third World countries; rather, it must be allowed to carry on as it sees fit. As one Monsanto executive put it, shortly after the Bhopal disaster: "Like it or not, we are operating in a world economy, and there is no turning back the clock of overseas investment."[29] Or, or course, on how that business is conducted.

After the disaster, *Business Week* editorialized that U.S. corporations "must insist on a continuing role in hiring, training and supervision in lands where the level of technological sophistication falls short of U.S. standards...Foreign governments, for their part, should swallow their nationalistic fervor and insist both on continuing hands-on involvement by the multinationals and on the best possible equipment for protecting their workers and neighboring communities."[30] The July 1985 agreement between IBM and the Mexican government is a clear example of U.S. capital's post-Bhopal agenda in the Third World. The Mexican government, facing severe economic problems, agreed to ignore its foreign investment law, which stipulates that foreign-affiliated companies can operate in Mexico only if majority ownership is in Mexican hands, and allow IBM to set up its own, 100 percent-owned facility. IBM agreed to increase the size of its investment in return. Noting that IBM was also interested in breaking into the Indian market, one business analyst stated, "Clearly, I.B.M. is in the midst of making a political statement, not only to the Southern Hemisphere but to India. I.B.M. wants to be in every country, and there are the terms and conditions under which they will play."[31]

_____

In contrast to the U.S.'s callous disinterest and defense of the status quo following the disaster, people in Bhopal and throughout India were stunned by the suddenness and magnitude of the December 3 slaughter. But for many, this shock rapidly gave way to intense anger. Contrary to statements in the U.S. press that the Indian people "don't really comprehend" what had happened,[32] millions understand perfectly well and know who is responsible. "Killer Carbide!," a slogan that arose spontaneously in the slums of Bhopal, succinctly expressed their outrage.

There were instances of mass protest, aimed at both Union Carbide and the Indian government. The day after the massacre, several thousand Bhopal residents tried to storm the factory. Plant officials and police guarding the plant, hopelessly outnumbered, only succeeded in turning the crowd away by telling them that another poisonous gas leak was in progress.

During December and January there were marches to and sit-ins at the residence of the Chief Minister of Madhya Pradesh; demonstrators marched in front of the Carbide factory, now protected by the Indian government; and on January 3, 1984, there was a large march in Bhopal of 10,000, including many slum dwellers never before involved in political action. Various forms of political agitation – for medical relief, compensation, and some for expropriating Union Carbide of India – continued through the summer of 1985.

Newspaper editorials denounced the negligence of Union Carbide, the lax complicity of the responsible authorities in India, and the multinationals' practice of dumping inferior technology and dangerous chemicals upon the Third World. One Bombay newspaper editorialized that, "The Multinational bastards of Union Carbide had transformed the entire city into a Nazi concentration camp," covering Bhopal with the "gas used by Hitler to massacre the Jews."[33] The disaster sparked widespread debate throughout India on issues ranging from the environmental hazards plaguing the country to the nature and direction of India's economic development and its relationship to foreign capital.

People in Bhopal's slums had received a traumatic jolt: "We were laborers and were trying to raise our families," said Nafisubi Ali. "Then we were suddenly under the trap of death by this killer gas." Slum dwellers expressed rage – at both Union Carbide for perpetrating the mass murder, and the Indian authorities for allowing it to happen. "Our country is a slave country," says Ramesh Sen, a load carrier and resident of Bhopal for 13 years. "And our government officials are simply purchased."

Ganesh War condemned the government for misinforming and misleading the people of India. "And besides this misinforming and misleading, the government is playing a nasty game, to save Union Carbide and companies like it in India." A self-educated poet who writes "about workers' destinies not only in my country but all over the world," Ganesh War describes how seeing thousands die has caused his individual grief to be merged into the collective grief of the whole community, and the world beyond. "It is not a question only of Union Carbide," he concludes, "but all the Union Carbides in India and the world."

But the Indian government's reaction to the massacre was quite low key and in keeping with efforts to dissipate popular outrage and preserve the country's links with foreign capital. In fact, India's relations with the industrial powers not only remained firmly in place, but in the case of the U.S. continued to improve. Speaking in New York on December 10, 1984, India's ambassador to the U.S. said that both governments were trying "to contain the damage," and that "I know the two Governments are in close touch with each other trying to maintain an even atmosphere even though there is this enormous public sense of dismay and even outrage."[34] When Prime Minister Rajiv Gandhi visited Bhopal on the evening of December 4, he refused to blame Union Carbide for the disaster. Instead, he implicitly blamed India, saying that it was a "cruel reminder" that Indian environmental regulations were faulty and that the fundamental problem was really urban overcrowding caused by rural migration.[35]

In April 1985, Gandhi spoke at a conference of businessmen from twenty-seven countries, held in New Delhi, and urged them to step up their investments in India, assuring them that his government was committed to opening up India to the world market.[36] Of the record 730 foreign collaboration agreements signed in 1984, 101 were with U.S. corporations, more than with any other country.[37]

In May 1985, an agreement was signed between the two countries allowing India to use sophisticated U.S. technology for business and military purposes.[38] Earlier that month, a high-level delegation from the U.S. Defense Department visited India to explore the possibility of selling it U.S. military hardware, something that hasn't been done for two decades.[39] In June 1985, Gandhi visited the U.S. and, according to all the press reports, had a very cordial discussion with President Reagan.[40] Bhopal was not discussed. According to the U.S. State Department, "it wasn't on our agenda and it wasn't on his."[41]

On the other hand, because of the politically volatile situation in India and the mass anger following the gassing of Bhopal, a certain amount of nationalist posturing was a political necessity for the Indian government – both in terms of preserving its own power domestically and in terms of its relations with foreign capital as well. The Carbide plant was shut down and seized by the Indian authorities, and Chief Minister Singh refused UCIL's offer of $840,000 in aid, saying, "I am not prepared to beg."[42]

Warren Anderson, who had gone to Bhopal right after the disaster, and five UCIL officials were arrested on a variety of criminal negligence charges. But this whole episode, originally designed to cover over the Indian government's history of collaboration with Union Carbide and to assuage public anger, ended up underscoring its continued collaboration and dependence.

To begin with, the Madhya Pradesh government couldn't come up with a cohesive legal explanation for why Anderson was arrested, stating instead that he had been detained to preserve law and order in Bhopal and for his own protection. Then Anderson was "jailed" – at Union Carbide's posh guest house overlooking Lake Bhopal. After a strong protest was reportedly registered by the U.S. chargé d'affaires in New Delhi, Anderson was released, just six hours after being "arrested," on $2,100 bail, even though he had been detained on nonbailable offenses. In fact, in India ordinarily any release on bail is conditional upon the accused reappearing in court; Anderson was released on condition he leave the country (which he had every intention of doing anyway). Finally, upon his release, an Indian government plane was put at Anderson's disposal. As Bombay's *Economic & Political Weekly* trenchantly noted, "Tragedy has been quickly followed by farce in Bhopal."[43]

The Indian authorities also tried to restore a calm atmosphere by downplaying the magnitude of the disaster, an approach paralleling Union Carbide's in certain respects. On December 4, Rajiv Gandhi assured the people of the city that the town's air, food, and water were safe, even though tests weren't to begin until the next day.[44] In the ensuing months, Bhopal was treated, in the words of Dr. Vinod Raina of Eklavya (Institute for Educational Research and Innovative Action), to "such amusingly nonsensical pronouncements by our esteemed official scientists that Bhopal 'water is safe, but boil it before you drink,' or 'vegetables are safe, but wash them before you cook – anyway, they will be rendered safe once cooked!' "[45]

The Indian government also instituted a virtual clampdown on any but the most general information regarding the disaster, designed not only to hide its own culpability but, more importantly, to maintain political control. The government which had been so lax when it came to regulating Union Carbide now showed itself to be highly organized when it came to keeping relevant information secret. Nothing of substance was available to the public: not the Union Carbide records that had been seized immediately after the disaster nor any results from the ongoing CBI investigation of it; not records of the licensing agreement nor any other government dealings with the company; nor the results of any of the air and water sampling tests that had been conducted in Bhopal; nor detailed medical records of the victims. As one newspaper put it, a gas leak may have been acceptable, but a news leak would be intolerable.

Newsmen were asked not to "play this thing up because it would create a lot of confusion and panic among the people," recalled Ashok Verma of United News of India in Bhopal. "The government said that the gas had already leaked and had whatever effect it was going to have. 'We're taking care of that,' they said, 'but creating panic will add to the problem.' "[46]

Astonishingly, given its declared interest in determining

exactly what had caused the disaster, the government also proposed destroying all the remaining MIC, making the testing of it impossible. This plan was stopped only by a petition of a private citizen to the High Court, demanding that some 15 kilograms be saved for examination.[47]

While the Indian government has promised to reveal all when the investigation is complete, or the case goes to court, the fact that both Union Carbide and the Indian government are angling for an out-of-court settlement (in part precisely to avoid any damaging exposure to either party) raises the possibility that much of the relevant information may never see the light of day. One Indian official said that the CBI report may be considered classified and may never be made public.[48]

But these efforts notwithstanding, maintaining control of the situation in Bhopal was easier said than done. In addition to the various demonstrations, "Operation Faith" − the government's mid-December 1984 effort to neutralize the remaining MIC at the Bhopal plant − revealed some of the problems the authorities were up against.

"People's faith has been rudely shaken by the events of the last few days," declared Chief Minister Singh. "That faith has to be restored. It shall be restored and none but God himself will see to it."[49] Restoring faith meant safely disposing of the remaining MIC, and assuring the population that the government was in complete control. But the method chosen to neutralize the MIC was converting it into Sevin − in other words, to operate the factory once again. Moreover, Union Carbide's Warren Woomer, the former plant manager, and several of the "arrested" Bhopal factory executives − some of the same people involved in the disaster in the first place − were going to supervise the operation. None of this, of course, reassured the people of Bhopal.

Elaborate safety measures were put in place, including helicopters flying overhead to spray the plant with water, wetting down the area surrounding the plant, and hanging sheets of damp burlap around the plant − all to neutralize any escaping MIC. A list of do's and don'ts in the event of an emergency was published in local papers. Evacuation camps were set up outside of town. Meanwhile chief minister Singh told the people of Bhopal, "There is no cause for panic and I repeat there is no reason to evacuate the city," and at the same time portrayed his decision to remain in Bhopal during "Operation Faith" as an act of courage. "No mortal can play God," he declared, "but we can certainly walk in the shadow of His grace and benediction fearlessly."[50]

But what all these safety precautions ended up doing was reviving nightmares of the deadliness of MIC. Four hundred thousand residents of Bhopal demonstrated their faith in Union Carbide and the Indian government by evacuating Bhopal *en masse* during "Operation Faith," leaving it a virtual ghost town. They returned only after the plant was once again shut down.

The state government also instituted a relief effort as part of preserving public order and confidence, declaring 10,000 rupees (approximately $770) compensation for every death, to be paid to the victims' relatives; 2,000 rupees *ex gratia* relief to the severely affected; and between 100 and 1,000 rupees to the moderately affected. Wheat, rice, sugar, edible oil, and milk were also distributed without cost to those affected by the gas. However, this relief effort was both limited and plagued by bureaucratic inefficiency and an official attitude which, as one journalist put it, "treats the victims like beggars, who may avail of the magnanimity of the government. . . in whatever form it thinks fit."[51] In some ways, the aid became a new source of discontent rather than increasing support for the authorities.

Many relatives of the dead, entitled to compensation, complained of difficulty in getting a death certificate, and getting the run-around when trying to confirm a relative's death without one. "They all say come back after two or three days and it will be taken care of," one resident said, "but nothing ever happens." By mid-June 1985, only 851 survivors of the deceased had received compensation.[52] And of course the government's estimate that only 1,754 had died in the disaster means that thousands of relatives will never get compensation.

Cash relief for the gas victims was suspended soon after the disaster. Since its resumption a few months later, few victims have received aid, and the amounts have been very small for those who have. As of mid-June 1985, only 946 severely affected persons had received an average of $118 each; 13,906 moderately affected people had received an average of $16 each; and 4,472 families with annual incomes below $500 received an *ex gratia* payment of $125. By the end of May 1985, the total relief expenditure, including compensation and food distribution, came to $13.75 million – an average of 38 cents per day per gas victim.[53]

Most of the seriously affected victims are unable to work, and with no jobs or government job rehabilitation programs in sight, they have been forced to turn to money lenders to tide them over, or to beg in the streets. Many have gone deeply into debt to pay for needed items. Many, dissatisfied by the treatment they have received at the free government hospitals and clinics, have had to turn to expensive private practitioners. Usury, with interest rates as high as 50 percent, is flourishing. One former Bhopal resident, who returned to the city in June 1985, said that unemployment in Bhopal was running between 30 and 40 percent and the neighborhoods surrounding Union Carbide had been turned into "colonies of beggars."[54]

The food distribution program included not only the victims, but half the population of Bhopal – 400,000 people or twice the estimated number of people affected in the gassing, an obvious political manuever to gain support for the government. When asked why free food had been given to so many, instead of concentrating the relief effort to make sure there would be enough food for the victims, the head of the state government's relief effort said, "The government would like to be generous in that [food distribution] instead of leaving out any needy persons." In the summer of 1985, milk and edible oil were eliminated from the food relief program.[55]

On June 25, 1985, several thousand people in Bhopal, mostly gas victims, staged a demonstration for adequate relief and treatment, and also employment. The government police and soldiers responded with a *lathi** charge, beating scores of demonstrators and arresting 21. Government officials worried aloud about the angry, confrontational mood of the demonstrators, and they claimed that the leaders of the demonstration were agents for Union Carbide.[56] Their logic was that since the demonstrators criticized the government's role in the disaster, and its relief measures in its aftermath, they must therefore be pro-Carbide.

---

*Long clubs

The official outcome of the Bhopal disaster is being decided in the courts and through back room negotiations. On April 8, 1985, the Indian government filed suit against Union Carbide in a U.S. court, and on June 28, 1985, a "consolidated" suit, combining slightly over 100 actions by U.S. lawyers, was also filed against Carbide in the U.S. Both demand billions in damages from Union Carbide on behalf of the victims of the December 3 gassing. Their essential reason for filing in the U.S. is to be able to tap into UCC's $10 billion in assets − over 100 times larger than those of UCIL − and to obtain a larger, quicker settlement in U.S. courts than probably would be possible in India. The legal justification for filing in the U.S. is the parent's majority ownership and its design and control of its Bhopal operation.

Union Carbide's response has been a study in imperiousness. The corporation has refused to accept any legal responsibility at all for the disaster. "The corporation did nothing that either caused or contributed to the accident," Warren Anderson told Carbide stockholders, "and if it comes to litigation we will vigorously defend that position."[57] On July 31, 1985, it filed to dismiss lawsuits filed against it in U.S. courts on the grounds that a U.S. forum was "inappropriate," and the case should instead be tried in India.

Union Carbide argues that India is the appropriate forum for the case because all the evidence and witnesses are in India; because the company involved, UCIL, is an Indian company that operates under Indian laws and regulations; because a settlement reached in U.S. courts may not be legally recognized in India, and thus be unenforceable; and because Bhopal's victims can seek recompense in India's courts (that is, if victims have no legal recourse in their own country to the actions of a U.S. concern this can be an argument for allowing a suit to be heard in the U.S., but in India, they do have such recourse).[58]

These arguments are specious on a number of counts. Much evidence actually resides in the U.S. − in the files at corporate headquarters in Danbury. While UCIL is located in India and is formally governed by Indian regulations, the principles of its operation were established in and are controlled from Danbury. Shifting the trial to India would, at the very least, hinder and in all likelihood prevent relevant records from being subpoenaed from

Danbury, as UCC could claim it was not within the jurisdiction of the Indian courts. In fact, moving the trial venue to India would in effect be an acceptance of Union Carbide's argument that the disaster was solely the responsibility of the subsidiary.

While Union Carbide's arguments appear to be motivated by respect for Indian sovereignty, they really boil down to the claim that U.S. capital should be allowed to operate in any country in the world, while being responsible to no one but itself. And Union Carbide is explicit about defending the interests of all U.S. multinationals in this regard. The corporation argues that if its victims in Bhopal are allowed to sue in the U.S., "Numerous so-called 'multinational' corporations, like Union Carbide, with interests in locally run companies conducting business in countries throughout the world," could also be subject to lawsuits in the U.S. It states, "The courts of the United States do not sit as world courts to decide foreign controversies arising in foreign lands brought by foreign citizens or their governments. . . Otherwise, the courts of the United States would soon be overwhelmed by litigation from all parts of the globe by foreign citizens and their governments seeking to take advantage of our judicial system, judges, juries, standards of value and taxpayers."[59] Indeed they might, given, among other things, the fact that Western capital routinely exports deadly processes and products to the Third World.

Union Carbide also contends that India is the appropriate forum because "trial in the United States would create insurmountable problems of communicating with Indian claimants, half a world away, who are unfamiliar with the American legal system, who do not speak English and in many, if not most, cases are not able to read or write in any language."[60] But then Union Carbide lawyers in India turn around and try to have many of the suits against the company dismissed there on the grounds that the plaintiffs are illiterate! The April 1985 issue of the *American Lawyer* reports that some 2,000 suits were filed against Union Carbide by gas victims in Bhopal, many seeking interim relief. Union Carbide lawyers have opposed every one of these suits on every legal and procedural technicality they could come up with – including the plaintiffs' illiteracy. Carbide lawyers told the Indian judge that "the plaintiffs are illiterate and do not understand the contents of the affidavits on which they have placed their thumb prints. Therefore...the complaints must be thrown out."[61]

In reading Union Carbide's arguments concerning Indian illiteracy, one cannot help but be struck by the parallels between it and the corporation's overall effort to blame the disaster on Indian backwardness, and the racist undertones of both. Carbide's argument that the case should be heard in India since most of the witnesses only speak Hindi is also ironic considering the fact that even when operating in Bhopal, the corporation failed to translate vital operating manuals into Hindi so that workers could better understand the processes at the Bhopal plant and operate it more safely.

The corporation also states, "Indeed, the practical impossibility for American courts and juries, imbued with U.S. cultural values, living standards and expectations, to determine damages for people living in the slums or 'hutments' surrounding the UCIL plant in Bhopal, India, by itself confirms that the Indian forum is overwhelmingly the most appropriate. Such abject poverty and the vastly different values, standards and expectations which accompany it are commonplace in India and the third world. They are incomprehensible to Americans living in the United States."[62]

Union Carbide is apparently worried that U.S. juries may not appreciate just how "cheap" life is in the Third World. But it, and the major media, seems to have those calculations well in hand. One *Wall Street Journal* column reports that "an American's life is worth about $500,000. But setting monetary value on the damage inflicted [in Bhopal], U.S. courts will take into account the differences between U.S. and Indian costs and standards of living. Indian per capita gross national product is only about 1.7% of the U.S. figure....Thus a court might award only $8,500 for an Indian's death."[63]

Union Carbide states that its offer for an out-of-court settlement "ranks with or exceeds all applicable standards, both in India and the United States. A $100 million settlement...would be enough to pay heirs of each decedent the equivalent of more than 100 years of annual income, and each of the reported serious injuries approximately 20 years annual income in Bhopal." This offer was based on a calculation of $127 as the average annual income in India.[64] *Business Week* decried these monetary calculations as "unseemly."[65] Unseemly they certainly are, but they also quite accurately represent imperialism's reduction of all human life to cash terms.

While so far there has been little apparent progress in resolving the dispute, and while both parties have their own particular, and conflicting, interests, they also share powerful common interests that could lead to an out-of-court settlement. Both agree that the most favorable solution is to throw token money at Bhopal's survivors. They only differ over how much. Union Carbide has reportedly been offering about $100 million – about half its reported liability insurance coverage. The Indian government reportedly "could not accept much less than $1 billion for political reasons."[66]

Both Union Carbide and the Indian government prefer an out-of-court settlement, and negotiations to that end are presently in progress. More than the money that Carbide is hoping to save or the speed with which the Indian government hopes to obtain a settlement, resolving the dispute outside the courtroom is a means of avoiding the damaging political fallout and incriminating exposure of both parties that a prolonged court case could entail. As far as Union Carbide and the Indian government are concerned, it is best that the full story of the Bhopal massacre remain buried in corporate and official vaults.

Was the disaster in Bhopal an accident, as it generally has been referred to in the U.S. media? Yes, in the sense that it was not inevitable that such a disaster should take place in Bhopal; and nothing predetermined the disaster's timing, or the precise sequence of events involved. But in a more fundamental sense, the disaster was not accidental: the logic of profit maximization and imperial domination shaped all the various components of the catastrophe – from the plant's design and location, to its day-to-day operational procedures and whole history, to the way the corporation reacted on the night of horror itself, to its actions in the wake of the gassing. In this sense, the disaster in Bhopal was not so much a tragedy as a crime; not so much a "unique combination of unusual events" as a horrifying and concentrated illustration of the essential operation of imperialism; not so much an accident as a massacre.

Union Carbide is not a particularly callous or unsafe company, an egregious exception to U.S. industry standards.[67] It is a reputable U.S. corporation, a pillar of the U.S. business community. Apparently the corporation's safety record was even comparable to, perhaps somewhat better than, other U.S. multinationals. This simply points to the fact that deeper forces shaped the disaster in Bhopal than the negligence of one corporation.

The massacre in Bhopal has largely faded from the headlines in the U.S. In fact, news of Bhopal began to fade within mere weeks of its occurrence, long before its true story had been told. There are powerful forces, including Union Carbide, the U.S. chemical industry, the U.S. media, and the U.S. and Indian governments, who have tried, and will continue to try, to relegate this crime to obscurity. But it won't be an easy task. The massacre in Bhopal struck a raw nerve in people the world over. It will not soon be forgotten. Or forgiven.

Endnotes

1 | The Night of Horror

1. "India Disaster: Chronicle of a Nightmare," *New York Times,* 10 December 1984.
2. Ivan Fera, "The Day After," *The Illustrated Weekly of India* (Bombay), 30 December 1984, pp. 10-11.
3. Ibid., p. 11.
4. "Top Safety Steps Claimed," *Free Press Journal* (Bhopal City edition), 4 December 1984; information from *Navbharat Times* cited in Fera, "The Day After," p. 11.
5. Talmiz Ahmad, Consul Commerce, Indian Consulate, New York, telephone interview with author, 8 August 1985.

2 | Design for Disaster

1. Union Carbide Corporation, "Bhopal Methyl Isocyanate Incident Investigation Team Report, March 1985" (report presented at Union Carbide Corporation's 20 March 1985 press conference, Danbury, CT), p. i. (Hereafter Union Carbide Corporation will be cited as UCC; this particular report as UCC, "Bhopal Incident Report.")

2. UCC, "Union Carbide Chairman Testifies Before Congressional Sub-committees" (press release), 14 December 1984.

3. Cited in "India's Night of Death," *Time,* 17 December 1984, p. 24.

4. UCC, "Opening Remarks – Warren M. Anderson, Chairman, Union Carbide Corporation, Press Conference, March 20, 1985" (mimeographed handout), p. 2.

5. UCC, "Van Mynen Presentation – Bhopal MIC Incident – March 1985, Press Conference – March 20, 1985" (mimeographed handout), p. 2.

6. "Bhopal is Still a Mystery," *New York Times,* 21 March 1985.

7. UCC, "Opening Remarks – Warren M. Anderson," p. 2.

8. UCC, *Annual Report 1984,* p. 5.

9. "Chemical-Plant Safety is Still Just Developing in Developing Nations," *Wall Street Journal,* 13 December 1984.

10. "Chemical Safety in Developing Countries: the Lessons of Bhopal," *Chemical & Engineering News (C&EN),* 8 April 1985, p. 10. In February *C&EN* wrote, "The direct blame falls on the managers of the plant" ("People of India Struggle Toward Appropriate Response to Tragedy," in "Bhopal: A *C&EN* Special Issue," *C&EN,* 11 February 1985, p. 16).

11. The *New York Times* series: "The Bhopal Disaster: How It Happened," 28 January 1985; "The Disaster in Bhopal: Workers Recall Horror," 30 January 1985; "Disaster in Bhopal: Where Does Blame Lie?" 31 January 1985; "The Disaster in Bhopal: Lessons for the Future," 3 February 1985. (Hereafter, each of these articles will be referred to by the second part of its title.)

12. "All the World Gasped," *Time,* 17 December 1984, p. 20. The *New York Times* editorialized, "In Bhopal, technology has showed its grimmest face. . . . Has technology outrun the capacity to control it?"; and warns against a rush to judgment against Union Carbide: "But in so extended a causal chain, blame may prove harder to fix than at first appearances" ("Risk and Blame at Bhopal," 9 December 1984, sec. E).

13. UCC, *Annual Report 1984,* pp. 40, 1, 18.

14. In 1905 UCC was called National Carbon. In 1934 The Eveready Company (India) was incorporated; in 1959 it changed its name to Union Carbide India Limited (UCIL, "Hexagon" [special publication commemorating UCIL's fiftieth anniversary], June 1984). UCIL's size from Centre for Monitoring Indian Economy (CMIE), *Basic Statistics Relating to the Indian Economy – Vol. 1: All India, August 1983* (Bombay: Centre for Monitoring Indian Economy, 1983), "Table 15.17: CMIE Listing of Top Two Hundred Fifty Industrial Units of India." (Hereafter, this reference is cited as CMIE, *Basic Statistics, 1983.*)

15. Statement of Ronald Wishart, vice president for government relations, UCC, before U.S. House Committee on Foreign Affairs, Subcommittee on Asian and Pacific Affairs, 12 December 1984, "The Implications of the Industrial Disaster in Bhopal India," 98th Congress, 2d sess. (Washington, D.C.: U.S. Government Printing Office,

1985), p. 34 (hereafter cited as House Subcommittee on Asian and Pacific Affairs, "Implications of Bhopal Disaster").
16. UCC, "Methyl Isocyanate" (UCC internal publication no. F-41443A-7/76, 1976), pp. 1, 25, 26, 27. The Material Safety Data Sheet, reprinted in "Methyl Isocyanate," states that the overexposure to MIC "may cause skin burns on contact. Vapors are extremely irritating and cause chest pain, coughing, and choking. May cause fatal pulmonary edema. Repeated exposure may cause asthma" (p. 27). (This document is reprinted in U.S. House Committee on Energy and Commerce, Subcommittee on Health and the Environment, "Hazardous Air Pollutants," 98th Congress, 2d sess., December 14, 1984 [Washington, D.C.: U.S. Government Printing Office, 1985, Serial No. 98-192].)
"Methyl Isocyanate" also states, "Water reacts exothermically to produce heat and carbon dioxide. As a result, the pressure in the tank will rise rapidly if methyl isocyanate is contaminated with water. This reaction may begin slowly, especially if there is no agitation, but it will become violent" (p. 9).
The operating manual for UCC's Bhopal factory states that MIC is "highly toxic and flammable," and "like phosgene, from which it is made, MIC also reacts violently with water, and care should be taken to exclude water from the system. Water and air contact with the process stream is to be avoided at all cost" (V.K. Behl et al., "Operating Manual Part I, Methyl Isocyanate Unit" [internal manual produced by Union Carbide India Limited, Agricultural Products Division, Bhopal, October 1978], p. 128).
17. "Bhopal: What Really Happened?," *Business India* (Bombay), 25 February–10 March 1985, pp. 102–116. Most of this description of the beginning of the disaster is based on the account appearing in *Business India,* which my investigation convinced me was the most accurate to date.
The overall sequence of events on the evening of 2–3 December is generally agreed upon and has been widely reported in the Indian press, including *Business India*; *Times of India* (New Delhi and Bombay); "City of Death," *India Today* (New Delhi), 31 December 1984, pp. 4–21; "The Guinea-Pig Controversy," *NOW* (New Delhi), January 1985, pp. 42–53; as well as in the *New York Times* series and UCC's "Bhopal Incident Report."
18. The CBI's confirmation of the existence of the jumper line has been reported in "Bhopal Probe Assails Carbide," *Newsday,* 12 February 1985; and "The Cover-Up–Why Union Carbide Should Be Thrown Out of India," *Sunday* (Calcutta), 7–13 April 1985, p. 19. The jumper's existence was also confirmed by the investigation of an international team of trade unionists. See International Confederation of Free Trade Unions (ICFTU) and International Federation of Chemical, Energy and General Workers Unions (ICEF), "The Trade Union

Report on Bhopal" (Geneva: ICFTU and ICEF, July 1985), pp. 7-8 (hereafter cited as ICFTU, "Trade Union Report"). UCC confirmation is cited in "Labor Report on Bhopal Cites Plant Modification," *New York Times,* 31 July 1985.

19. As I shall discuss in greater detail in chapter 7, UCC opposes the thesis that water entered tank 610 through the RVVH and the PVH as a result of water washing; instead arguing that, while it does not know for certain how water got in, the most probable route was the "direct introduction of water" into the tank through the process vent line, nitrogen line, or other piping. However, the company does admit that "Tank 610 could not be pressurized on November 30 and December 1, although nitrogen was reported to be flowing into the tank. It is possible that a vent valve was leaking or the rupture disc was not intact and the safety valve was leaking.... If nitrogen was indeed escaping, the escape route could also have provided a route of entry for water" (UCC, "Van Mynen Presentation," pp. 11-12).

20. 11,290-gallon estimate in UCC, "Bhopal Incident Report," p. 11; 13,000-gallon estimate in "How It Happened," *New York Times.*

21. UCC's "Methyl Isocyanate" states, "For safety reasons, size the tanks twice the volume required for storage. Use the added volume, in an emergency, for space to add inert diluent as a heat sink; addition of a diluent will not stop a reaction but will provide more time to control the problem. As an alternative, keep an empty tank available at all times. If the methyl isocyanate tank becomes contaminated or fails, transfer part or all the contents to the empty standby tank" (p. 7).

22. UCC, "Bhopal Incident Report," p. 13.

23. Ibid., p. 21.

24. UCC, "Methyl Isocyanate," p. 9.

25. UCC, "Bhopal Incident Report," p. 21.

26. Ibid., p. 23.

27. Ibid., pp. 11, 23. The *New York Times* reports, "Operators said they did not record the temperature of the tank. 'For a very long time we have not watched the temperature,' one worker said. 'There was no column to record it in the log books.'... Sometimes in the summer, operators said, the methyl isocyanate storage tank temperature indicator went off the scale, which was 25 degrees Centigrade at the maximum, or 77 degrees Fahrenheit" ("Workers Recall Horror," *New York Times*).

28. UCC, "Bhopal Incident Report," pp. 11-12. The *New York Times* reports that second shift operators did record the 2 psig pressure in tank 610, and that the third shift operator noticed the rise to 10 psig, but "thought nothing of it," because it was "still a relatively normal pressure," and because the plant's instrumentation was often faulty ("Workers Recall Horror," *New York Times*).

29. "The Guinea-Pig Controversy," *Now,* p. 49; "How It Happened" and "Workers Recall Horror," *New York Times.*

30. UCC, "Bhopal Incident Report," p. 24.
31. "How It Happened," *New York Times*
32. "Workers Recall Horror," *New York Times*. UCC's "Investigation Report" states that workers "turned on the fixed firewater monitors and directed them to the stack and the MIC process area to knock down the MIC vapor as much as possible. In a test subsequent to the event with two monitors in service, water reached beyond the top of the stack" (p. 12). This is contradicted by the *New York Times* as well as *India Today* ("City of Death," p. 9), and in any event the water spray did little to control the toxic gas release.
33. UCC, "Investigation Report," p. 24.
34. Cited in "An Unending Search for Safety," *Time*, 17 December 1984, p. 35.
35. UCC, "Carbide Chairman Testifies."
36. John Macdonald, Assistant Secretary for Union Carbide Corporation, "Affidavit in Support of Union Carbide's Motion to Dismiss on Grounds of *Forum Non Conveniens*" (deposition filed in United States District Court, Southern District of New York), 31 July 1985, pp. 4–5.

    Even if UCC's allegations were true, which they are not, it could be difficult for them to blame design failures on India's technological backwardness. The company that assisted in the construction and detailed design, Humphreys & Glasgow Consults Pvt. Ltd. of Bombay, is itself part of a multinational: its parent is based in London and has recently been bought by the Ensearch Corporation of Dallas ("How It Happened," *New York Times*).
37. Edward Munoz, "Affidavit of Edward Munoz" (deposition filed with the Judicial Panel on Multidistrict Litigation, New York), 28 January 1985, p. 2.
38. The Bhopal factory works manager, Mukund, was asked, "Is it true that UCC designed the entire plant and also took the responsibility for checking each piece of equipment for its quality?" He replied, "Yes, I should think so" ("A Deadly Delay in Bhopal," *Times of India*, 19 December 1984).
39. Kelley Drye & Warren (attorneys for Union Carbide Corporation), "Memorandum of Law in Support of Union Carbide Corporation's Motion to Dismiss These Actions on the Grounds of *Forum Non Conveniens*" (filed in United States District Court, Southern District of New York), 31 July 1985, p. 45 (hereafter cited as Kelley Drye & Warren, "Memorandum in Support of UCC").
40. "Government Responsibility for Bhopal Gas Tragedy," *Economic and Political Weekly (E&PW)* (Bombay), 15 December 1985, p. 2109.
41. Dr. B. P. Srivastava, head UCIL Research and Development Lab, Bhopal, interview with author, 25 February 1985. While UCC had been manufacturing MIC since the late 1950s, it only began using MIC to manufacture Sevin pesticide in 1973 ("Bhopal: A *C&EN* Special Issue," *C&EN*, p. 32).

42. UCC's "Methyl Isocyanate" states, "With bulk systems, contamination is more likely than with tightly-sealed drums" (p. 9).
43. "Government Responsibility for Bhopal Gas Tragedy," *E&PW,* p. 2109.
44. ICFTU, "Trade Union Report," p. 15.
45. Munoz, "Affidavit," pp. 2–3.
46. "Bhopal: A *C&EN* Special Issue," *C&EN,* p. 32.
47. S. Kumaraswami, UCIL resident manager, New Delhi, interview with author, 13 March 1985, New Delhi.
48. "Plant Design Badly Flawed," *Times of India,* 27 December 1984.
49. "The Catastrophe at Bhopal," *Business India,* 17–30 December 1984, p. 76.
50. U.S. Department of Labor, Occupational Safety and Health Administration (OSHA), "Inspection Report Union Carbide Corporation, Institute, West Virginia" (photocopied OSHA report), 6 December 1984–13 February 1985, p. 4 (hereafter cited as OSHA, "Institute Inspection Report").
51. Behl et al., "Operating Manual," p. 127. In full, it states, "Contamination of equipment is difficult to check as quick detection means are not available. The only way to determine if MIC is present is to vent or purge the equipment into the air. If odor or eye irritation is not detected, the MIC is not present. Obviously this must be done carefully to prevent over exposure."
52. According to the American Conference of Governmental Industrial Hygienists, Inc., MIC cannot be detected at 0.4 ppm, which is 20 times higher than MIC's threshold limit value (TLV) of 0.02 ppm. They report that at 2 ppm (100 times MIC's TLV), "no odor was detected but the subjects experienced irritation and lacrymation." The symptoms didn't become unbearable until 21 ppm (House Subcommittee on Health and the Environment, "Hazardous Air Pollutants," p. 493).
53. UCC, "Methyl Isocyanate," p. 25. It states, "Stringent precautions must be observed to eliminate any possibility of human contact with methyl isocyanate."
54. UCC Chemicals and Plastics (South Charleston, WV), "Operational Safety Survey – CO/MIC/Sevin Units, Union Carbide India Ltd., Bhopal Plant" (internal company report), May 1982, p. 10 (hereafter cited as UCC, "1982 Safety Survey"). The survey also notes, "Manual control of filling of the tank [MIC feed tank, not storage tank – ed.], with no instrumentation backup, creates a possibility of accidental overfilling" (p. 8).
55. Cited in "1982 Inspector Says Indian Plant Was Below U.S. Safety Standards," *New York Times,* 12 December 1984. It should be noted that Tyson was drawing attention to the differences between Bhopal and Institute – in contrast to earlier UCC statements that the two plants were identical – to reassure U.S. citizens that such a disaster

couldn't happen here. The 11 August 1985 leak at Institute demonstrated just how reliable these U.S. standards are. Tyson claimed that less instrumentation had been used in Bhopal in order to create jobs. The hollowness of this argument is demonstrated not only by the fact that a lack of instrumentation doesn't necessarily create more jobs, but also by the massive layoffs that occurred the year after his report.

56. Behl et al., "Operating Manual," pp. 79, 81.
57. U. Nanda, safety director, Bhopal plant, telephone interview with author, 2 March 1985, Bhopal.
58. "Plant Design Badly Flawed," *Times of India.*
59. UCC, "1982 Safety Survey," p. 6.
60. "Carbide Works to Reopen U.S. Plant," *New York Times,* 22 March 1985.
61. UCC, "Remarks of Jackson B. Browning, Press Conference – 20 March 1985" (mimeographed handout), p. 5. Browning explained that these changes didn't mean that Institute had been unsafe, rather the changes were an example of making the "MIC operation at Institute safer still. . . . Our safety programs and safety surveys are based on the premise that you can always do better."
62. Ibid., p. 1. "Could the same thing happen here?. . . We can confidently say: It can't happen here." On 25 January 1985, in response to charges that Institute was unsafe in light of the MIC leaks that had occurred over the past five years, Browning declared, "This plant is absolutely safe" ("Carbide Rebuts Charges," *Newsday,* 26 January 1985).
63. The information on the 11 August 1985 leak at UCC's Institute plant is taken from "Toxic Cloud Leaks at Carbide Plant in West Virginia," *New York Times,* 12 August 1985; "Carbide Blames a Faulty Design for Toxic Leak," *New York Times,* 13 August 1985; and "Carbide Computer Could Not Track Gas That Escaped," *New York Times,* 14 August 1985.
64. "An Unending Search for Safety," *Time,* 17 December 1985, p. 35. At the corporation's 20 March 1985 press conference, Chairman Anderson stated that "nothing could be further from the truth" than the assertion that UCC was making MIC in Bhopal because it was cheaper to produce there. "In fact, it's more expensive to make this product there than to make it in the U.S. and ship it all the way to India" (UCC, "Concluding Remarks – Warren M. Anderson, Chairman, UCC, Press Conference – March 20, 1985" [mimeographed handout], p. 4). Even if this were true, it is beside the point. The overall calculus of Carbide's operations – in this case its overall position in India and that country's potentially huge market in particular – determined process decisions, not the cost of one or another component.
65. Business Bulletin, *Wall Street Journal,* 27 June 1985. In 1984, Union Carbide reported spending $106 million for "protection of the environment and for compliance with federal, state and local anti-pollution regulations." This figure represented 4 percent of Carbide's

total capital spending for the year (which was slightly over half what it was in 1981), and 1.1 percent of its total turnover. (Environmental expenses from UCC, "Union Carbide Corporation 1984 10-K" [annual report submitted to the Securities and Exchange Commission, Washington, D.C.], p. 2; overall capital expenditures from UCC, *Annual Report 1984*, p. 1, and UCC, *Annual Report 1981*, p. 1.)

66. "Problem of Toxic Emissions," *New York Times*, 20 May 1985.
67. "Union Carbide Reports 33 More Leaks at U.S. Site," *New York Times*, 31 January 1985.
68. Testimony of and materials submitted by Perry Bryant, West Virginia – Citizen Action Group, to House Subcommittee on Health and the Environment, in "Hazardous Air Pollutants," pp. 162, 158. U.S. chemical plants are not designed to maximize safety in terms of the storage of dangerous chemicals either. For instance, a recent OSHA Report states that at the FMC plant in Middleport, New York, MIC is stored in a 42,000-gallon tank; at the DuPont chemical plant in LaPorte, Texas, MIC is stored in two 30,000-gallon tanks (OSHA, "Inspection Report, FMC – Middleport, New York," 18 December 1984– 13 February 1985, p. 5; and OSHA, "Inspection Report, E.I. DuPont de Nemours & Co., Inc., LaPorte, Texas," 18 December 1984–24 January 1985, p. 3 [both are photocopied OSHA reports]).
69. "Cause and Effect," *Far Eastern Economic Review*, 27 December 1984– 3 January 1985, p. 16.
70. UCC, "Union Carbide Says Process Safety Standards are 'Identical' at Bhopal and Institute Plants" (press release), 11 December 1984.
71. UCC, "Remarks of Jackson B. Browning," p. 3.
72. U.S. Environmental Protection Agency (EPA), "Multi-Media Compliance Inspection – Union Carbide Corporation, Institute, WV" (photocopied EPA report), 4 January 1985, section 2, p. 3 (hereafter cited as EPA, "Institute Compliance Report").
73. OSHA, "Institute Inspection Report," p. 6. OSHA also notes that MIC is "maintained at or below 0° C." and the "refrigeration system can maintain the MIC at a temperature of 0° C. or lower."
74. UCC, "Union Carbide Says Process Safety Standards are 'Identical.'"
75. U. Nanda, telephone interview with author; see also Thomas M. Gladwin and Ingo Walter, "Bhopal and the Multinational," *Wall Street Journal*, 16 January 1985.
76. OSHA, "Institute Inspection Report," pp. 6–7. UCC did not respond to a series of questions posed by this author concerning other safety-related differences between the Bhopal and Institute plants.
77. "Could It Happen in America?," *Newsweek*, 17 December 1984, p. 21. Here *Newsweek* is discussing the "Safer" computer system, the same type of system installed at Institute as part of the $5 million improvement plan. At this point it seems that the problem was in UCC's failure to purchase a program to track aldicarb oxime, rather than the Safer program per se. See "Carbide Leak Puts Chief of Safer in Lime-

light," *New York Times,* 15 August 1985.
78. See "Bhopal: A *C&EN* Special Issue," *C&EN,* p. 32; "The Catastrophe at Bhopal," *Business India,* 17–30 December 1984, p. 76.
79. "Lessons for the Future," *New York Times.*
80. Cited in "In the Aftermath of Bhopal, Anderson Speaks," *Hartford Courant,* 16 January 1985.
81. Munoz, "Affidavit," p. 3.
82. " 'Safety' Criteria for Extending UCIL Term," *Indian Express,* 7 December 1984. The article notes, "In its application in September 1982, UCIL sought extension on the ground that its parent company having 'experience in handling toxic chemicals over several years' would make available to UCIL 'the current knowledge and experiences in handling highly toxic materials' on a continuous basis. It said that 'continuous availability of data in this area will assist UCIL in fully protecting the plant personnel and properties.' UCIL further justified the extension on the ground that the U.S. firm would make available as a result of the collaboration, 'toxicology data on products produced besides antidotes and safety precautions.' "
83. Between 1970 and 1976 UCIL remitted over $2.3 million in technical know-how fees and royalties to UCC, along with over $4 million in dividends. In 1982 the figures were $474,000 and $1.43 million respectively (Lok Sabha [Indian Parliament in New Delhi], "Remittances Made by Foreign-Controlled Companies from 1970 to 1976" [Reply to Unstarred Question No. 4307 for 16.12.77 – photocopied document]); and UCIL, *Annual Report 1983,* p. 25). (Note: Throughout this book, wherever I have converted rupee amounts into U.S. dollars, I have used 13 rupees = one dollar, the approximate exchange rate as of this writing.)
84. CMIE, *Basic Statistics, 1983,* "Table 11.1: Estimated Stock of Scientific and Technical Personnel – 1950 to 1985."

3 | Procedures, Projections, and Danger in the Slums

1. Prepared Statement of James Gustave Speth, President, World Resources Institute, in House Subcommittee on Asian and Pacific Affairs, "Implications of Bhopal Disaster," pp. 47–48. He notes that UCIL has a 7 percent share of the Indian pesticide market. Indian pesticide use from 1966–67 to 1970–71 from CMIE, *Basic Statistics, 1983,* "Table 12.12-1: An Overall View of Recent Trends in Agricultural Inputs – 1966–67 to 1983–84."
2. "From Independence to Indira Gandhi," *Fortune India* (Bombay), February 1985, pp. 4–5.

3. CMIE, *Basic Statistics, 1983,* "Table 13.1: CSO's Estimates of Gross Value of Output and Inputs During 1970–71 to 1980–81." This decline in part reflected increased agricultural production, but it also reflected lagging – and continued low – farm incomes. In 1970–71 net income per farm family per year was $94; it rose to $154 in 1974–75, but was only $162 in 1980–81.

4. CMIE, *Basic Statistics, 1983,* "Table 12.12-1."

5. Cited in "Pesticide Plant Started as a Showpiece but Ran into Troubles," *New York Times,* 3 February 1985.

6. UCIL, *Annual Report 1983,* p. 25.

7. "Plant Undermanned, Run Down," *Times of India,* 1 January 1985.

8. "Pesticide Plant Started as Showpiece," *New York Times.*

9. "50 Years, and Showing Its Age," *Fortune India,* July 1984, p. 45.

10. Union Carbide, *Annual Report 1984,* p. 21.

11. See "Plant Undermanned, Run Down," *Times of India;* "Union Carbide Wanted to Sell Bhopal Plant," *Sunday Observer* (Bombay), 9 December 1984; "Pesticide Plant Started as a Showpiece," *New York Times.*

12. Memorandum of Agreement dated 14 May 1983, between UCIL Agricultural Products Division, Bhopal and Its Hourly Rated Employees (photocopy of union contract for Bhopal plant courtesy of EKLAVYA [Institute for Educational Research and Innovative Action], Bhopal), p. 4.

13. "Plant Undermanned, Run Down," *Times of India.*

14. ICFTU, "Trade Union Report," p. 10.

15. "City of Death," *India Today,* 31 December 1984, p. 10.

16. "Memorandum of Agreement," p. 2.

17. "Plant Undermanned, Run Down," *Times of India.*

18. ICFTU, "Trade Union Report," p. 10.

19. UCC, "1982 Safety Survey," p. 5; Behl et al., "Operating Manual," p. 103.

20. UCC, "Methyl Isocyanate," p. 9.

21. When asked in an interview with Praful Bidwai why the flare tower had been disconnected from the scrubber and why the pilot light had been turned off, works manager Mukund stated, "It's our normal practice. We do it when the plant [MIC production unit – ed.] is not running" ("A Deadly Delay in Bhopal," *Times of India,* 19 December 1984).

22. "Mismanagement Model," *Now* (New Delhi), January 1985, p. 46.

23. "Lessons for the Future," *New York Times.*

It should also be noted that while Union Carbide has stressed that its procedures were sound, but simply not followed, there are indications that some of the procedures themselves were flawed. Carbide emphasized that the MIC in tank 610 was contaminated with high levels of chloroform, and that the tank was supposed to be checked "each day it [MIC] is being produced," to detect such contamination, implying that the problem was created when UCIL employees failed to carry out such tests when the MIC, stored in tank 610, was produced (UCC, "Bhopal Incident Report," p. 8). But Dr. Varadarajan found after the disaster that Union Carbide didn't have an accurate means of determining the amount of chlorine and chlorine compounds present in MIC, indicating the problem was with the procedures themselves. Further, Carbide has emphasized the shutting off of the refrigeration unit and the fact that tank temperatures were between 15 and 20 degrees C., a central issue in its case for procedural violations being the heart of the disaster. But one of Carbide's own publications states that stored MIC should be maintained "below 15° C. and preferably at about 0° C." (UCC, "Methyl Isocyanate," p. 7), raising the possibility that on 2 December, the temperatures in tank 610 were actually within the specifications prescribed by Union Carbide, or very close to them. (In its "Bhopal Incident Report," UCC states, "The temperature of MIC in Tank 610 before the incident was at 15 to 20 degrees C. as compared to the requirement of about 0 degrees C." [p. 23]. The company doesn't explain this discrepancy with its earlier specifications.) UCC also contradicted its avowed policy on storage levels in MIC tanks. In its report, UCC states, "The liquid level in Tank 610 was near 70 percent of capacity, which is below the maximum operating level" (p. 11). Yet its publication, "Methyl Isocyanate," states, "For safety reasons, size the tanks twice the volume required for storage" (p. 7). This again illustrates how not only were some of its procedures flawed, but that the corporation did not pay strict attention to its declared safety practices at any level of operation. It should also be noted that the EPA states that some MIC tanks at the Institute plant are kept up to 80 percent full (EPA, "Institute Compliance Report," section 2, p. 2).

24. See Nancy Shute, Linda Sarrio, and Frank O'Donnell, "Temik Investigations" (photocopied collection of articles published by Network News Inc., 1983).
25. Dr. L. D. Loya, interview with author, 1 March 1985, Bhopal. (All subsequent quotes from Dr. Loya are from this interview unless otherwise cited.)
26. H. M. Zariwala, interview with author, 24 February 1985, Bhopal. (All subsequent quotes from Zariwala are from this interview unless otherwise cited.)
27. ICFTU, "Trade Union Report," p. 10.
28. Government of Madhya Pradesh, "Accidents in the Union Carbide, Bhopal" (mimeographed handout to press conference), 8 December 1984, Bhopal.
29. "Lessons for the Future," *New York Times.*
30. V. P. Gokhale, managing director UCIL, interview with author, 16 March 1985, Bhopal. (All subsequent quotes from Gokhale are from this interview unless otherwise cited.)

31. Indian Council of Medical Research (ICMR), New Delhi, "The Bhopal Disaster – Current Status (The First Nine Days) and Programme of Research" (photocopy of ICMR report), p. 2. On the cover it states, "This report is based on the visits made by the scientists from the National Institute of Occupational Health, National Institute of Nutrition, the Cytology Research Centre and the Director-General of the Indian Council of Medical Research between the 5th and 11th December."

32. UCC, "Bhopal Incident Report," pp. 11–12.

33. "Bhopal: What Really Happened?," *Business India,* 25 February–10 March 1985, p. 109.

    The essentials of this scenario were substantiated by *India Today* ("City of Death," 31 December 1984, p. 11); *Now* ("The 'Inside' Story," January 1985, p. 50); and, according to *Newsday,* by the Indian government ("Bhopal Probe Assails Carbide," 12 February 1985). None of the slum dwellers I talked to reported being awakened by an alarm; all told of being awakened by the burning or choking effects of the gasses.

34. "Workers Recall Horror," *New York Times.*

35. Fera, "The Day After," p. 11. Even two weeks after the disaster, works manager Mukund was still downplaying the toxicity of MIC. When asked whether he had stated MIC was "only an irritant, it is not fatal," he replied, "Well it depends on how one looks at it. See, in its effects, it is like tear gas, your eyes start watering. And you apply water, and you get relief" ("A Deadly Delay in Bhopal," *Times of India*).

36. Dr. Ranjit Singh, interview with author, 1 March 1985, Bhopal. (All subsequent quotes from Dr. Singh are from this interview unless otherwise cited.)

37. "West Virginia Officials Assailing Delay in Alert," *New York Times,* 13 August 1985.

38. Cited in "Toxic Cloud Leaks at Carbide Plant in West Virginia," *New York Times,* 12 August 1985.

39. Geraldine Cox, ABC News *Nightline,* 12 August 1985.

40. UCC, "Proposed Industrial Hygiene Monitoring Program for 1984" (UCC internal memo), 28 November 1983 (cited in House Subcommittee on Health and the Environment, "Hazardous Air Pollutants," pp. 523–33). The memo was addressed to, among others, Dr. Avashia.

41. "Carbide Asserts String of Errors Caused Gas Leak," *New York Times,* 24 August 1985.

42. Ibid.

43. "Union Carbide Says Bhopal Facility Should Have Been Shut Before Accident," *Wall Street Journal,* 21 March 1985.

    Gokhale advanced a similar argument, stating, "In any organization when you have fourteen factories the system of monitoring the fourteen factories . . . cannot be done by one person sitting in a central office. . . . These people are supposed to report to us periodically on *any* exceptions to the policies and procedures. If they do not report exceptions to the procedures it is assumed they are following them."

44. Robert Oldford, president of Union Carbide Agricultural Products Company, Inc., in UCC, "Union Carbide Corporation Calls for Conversion of Brazilian Methyl Isocyanate" (press release), 7 December 1984.

45. "Compliance with safety procedures is a local issue," said Warren Anderson at the company's 20 March 1985 press conference (cited in "Union Carbide's Inquiry Indicates Errors Led to India Plant Disaster," *New York Times*, 21 March 1985).

46. See UCC, *Annual Report 1984*, pp. 39, 40; Ed Van Den Ameele, UCC press spokesperson, telephone interview with author, 7 August 1985; UCIL, *Annual Report 1983*, p. 1; UCIL, *Prospectus*, 19 October 1981, pp. 5–7.

47. Edward Munoz, "Affidavit," pp. 2–3.

48. The *New York Times* quotes a former official as stating, "The line of communication was loud and clear. Any major safety issue, financial commitment or problem had to be cleared with Union Carbide Corporation." The *New York Times* states that, according to these officials, reports were sent between Bhopal and the U.S. every month, with more detailed reports each three to six months, and that "every major decision such as the annual budget was cleared with the American headquarters. . . and directives were often issued from the United States." Further, "the parent company also had the right to intervene in day-to-day affairs if it concluded that safety might be affected" ("U.S. Company Said to Have Had Control in Bhopal," *New York Times*, 28 January 1985).

49. Works manager Mukund stated that UCC was "fully aware" of the Bhopal factory's progress in implementing UCC safety and maintenance recommendations. "We have been sending periodic reports, every quarter. . . detailed reports. . . . They appear fully satisfied with our operation and maintenance practices. I think it's false to say that they did not approve of these" ("A Deadly Delay in Bhopal," *Times of India*).

   Business India ("Bhopal: What Really Happened?") reports that headquarters knew about the installation of the jumper line (p. 103); Dr. Varadarajan told the *New York Times* that his staff had been told by UCIL management that the refrigeration unit had been turned off "because the managers had concluded after discussions with American headquarters that the device was not necessary" ("How It Happened," *New York Times*).

   Gokhale said that UCIL and UCC "keep in very frequent communication relating to the safety performance of each of the plants." When asked why UCIL officials couldn't discuss the details of the subsidiary's relationship with UCC, Gokhale said, "I really don't know the answer to that one. I know that we are not discussing it publicly." While UCC claimed to have lost control of its subsidiary in safety matters, it obviously had the power to enforce an information clampdown.

50. "India Says Carbide Itself is Responsible," *New York Times,* 22 March 1985.
51. Quotes in this and the preceding two paragraphs from UCC, "1982 Safety Survey," cover memo and pp. 2, 5, 14, 20, 11, 6, 1.

UCC's Jackson Browning stated on 11 December 1984, "Subsequent progress reports from Union Carbide India Limited represented to Union Carbide Corporation that all problems uncovered in the 1982 survey had been taken care of. . . . We have no reason to believe that what was represented to us by Union Carbide India Limited did not in fact occur" (UCC, "Union Carbide's J. B. Browning Says Safety is an 'Ongoing' Process for Company Worldwide" [press release], 11 December 1984).

The safety committee at the Bhopal plant functioned in a similarly perfunctory fashion. According to safety director Nanda, it confined itself principally to such routine matters as audits of existing safety equipment, safety education, mock drills, safety shoes, and the like. Overall process and design, and even such key procedural decisions as shutting off the refrigeration unit, the flare, and the scrubber, weren't even discussed in the meeting of the central, plant-wide safety committee.

52. UCC, Engineering and Technology Services, South Charleston, WV, "Operational Safety/Health Survey—MIC II Unit, Institute Plant," 10 September 1984. (This internal UCC report is available in House Subcommittee on Health and the Environment, "Hazardous Air Pollutants," pp. 458–76.)
53. "Carbide Says It Averted Threat at U.S. Plant," *New York Times,* 26 January 1985. Gokhale stated he didn't know why UCC didn't send the report to UCIL.
54. Cited in "In the Aftermath of Bhopal, Anderson Speaks," *Hartford Courant,* 16 January 1985.
55. Directorate of Economics and Statistics, "Salient Facts of Madhya Pradesh" (Bhopal: Government of Madhya Pradesh, 1983), p. 6.
56. Ibid., pp. 11, 8; U.S. statistics from *Information Please Almanac 1985* (Boston: Houghton Mifflin Company, 1985), p. 82.
57. Department of Town and Country Planning, *Bhopal Development Plan* (Bhopal: Government of Madhya Pradesh, 1975), pp. 67–69.
58. UCC, "Union Carbide Reports No Previous Incidents of Multiple Deaths at Bhopal, India, Plant" (press release), 6 December 1984, p. 3.
59. "Carbide Execs: 'We Think We Can Handle This,' " *Chemical Week,* 2–9 January 1985, p. 6.
60. See Department of Town and Country Planning, *Bhopal Development Plan,* "Bhopal Sequence of Growth" diagram (no page number).

61. Ibid., pp. 67–69.
62. UCIL, "Brief History Agricultural Product Division, Union Carbide India Limited, Bhopal" (UCIL mimeograph). It states, "It was indeed a kind gesture on the part of the Government of Madhya Pradesh to have invited the Company to set up the factory at Bhopal and allocate the land at Berasia Road with a promise of generous supply of power, water and other essential items required for such a large scale manufacture."
63. Zariwala, interview with author. He said that, in the early to mid-1970s, UCIL had employed over 500 casual laborers in Bhopal, and after 1983 some 300 casual workers were laid off. In the U.S., wages comprise 28 percent of domestic sales; UCIL employee-related operating expenses are only 12.7 percent of sales (UCC, *Annual Report 1984*, p. 23; UCIL, *Annual Report 1983*, p. 15).
64. Madhya Pradesh Audyogik Vikas Nigam Limited (Industrial Development Corporation), "Directory of Existing Medium/Large Industrial Units of Madhya Pradesh" (Bhopal: 1984). A *Wall Street Journal* article states, "Aside from Union Carbide, all Bhopal has to-day is one smoky plant that presses straw into particle board, and a million or so terribly poor people" ("Death in Bhopal: Compensation Seems Not Quite the Point," 19 December 1984).
65. See, for example, "Slums Alongside Factories Inevitable, Experts Say," *New York Times*, 10 December 1984. The article never mentions the changes wrought by imperialism in the Third World countryside.

4 | The Gas Chamber

1. "Why Union Carbide Should Be Thrown Out," *Sunday*, p. 23.
2. UCC, "Union Carbide Employees Worldwide Express Concern and Sympathy" (press release), 6 December 1984.
3. ICMR, "The Bhopal Disaster – Current Status," pp. 2–4.
4. "Profit Against Safety," *E&PW*, 22–29 December 1984, p. 2150.
5. "Bhopal's Doctors Given High Praise," *New York Times*, 18 December 1984.
6. Dr. Heeresh Chandra, interview with author, 4 March 1985, Bhopal. (All subsequent quotations by Dr. Chandra are from this interview unless otherwise stated.)
7. Doctors from Bombay later studied 1,000 people in the railway colony, situated less than one mile from the Carbide factory, and their observations of the immediate reactions of those exposed to the gas also support the cyanide diagnosis. They reported that when subjects were suddenly exposed to the gas, some fainted or felt extremely

weak and became unconscious. Others vomited, defecated, and urinated involuntarily. Still others died within minutes of exposure. The doctors report that within one hour at the Bhopal railway station alone, 21 persons died, 200 were lying unconscious and the whole station was littered with around 600 suffering people lying among their own excreta. They report that, based on these observations and blood tests of the survivors, in patients who died within a few minutes of exposure, cyanide excess may have had a role (Dr. S. R. Kamat et al., "Preliminary Observations on Early Toxicity in Subjects Exposed to the Isocyanate Gas Leak Disaster at Bhopal" (unpublished paper), pp. 3–4, 12).

8. "Bhopal: What Really Happened?," *Business India*, p. 111. See also Fera, "The Day After," pp. 11–12, for a good account of the discovery of cyanide poisoning.

9. UCC, "From Union Carbide Corporation, U.S.A. – Treatment of MIC – Pulmonary Complication" (photocopy of UCC's 5 December 1984 telegram).

10. "Bhopal: What Really Happened?," *Business India*, p. 115.

11. "He Thought It Was Cyanide," *Free Press Journal*, 15 December 1984.

12. As mentioned in chapter 3, n. 40, Dr. Avashia had been sent an internal company memo on 28 November 1983, listing the principal toxins used at Institute, which produced a much wider range of chemicals than Bhopal. Neither "methyl-isocyanide" nor "methyl isocyanite" was on the list.

13. UCC, "Union Carbide Chairman Leads Team of Experts to Bhopal" (press release), 4 December 1984, p. 1.

14. "Carbide Misled Doctors," *Indian Express* (Bombay), 28 January 1985. The *Express* reports that Carbide passed out a statement at its 14 December 1984 press conference stating:

> "Methyl isocyanate is not a cyanide. They must be differentiated. Isocyanates are molecules containing the radical N.C.O., whereas cyanides contain the C.N. radical. MIC naturally degrades in the environment by reacting readily with water to become harmless substances, while cyanides do not react with water. These two substances have an entirely different effect on tissues and human health."

(This article was reproduced in Vivek Pinto and Stephen D. O'Leary, eds., *Reprints of Selected Documents on the December 1984 Union Carbide Chemical Incident* [San Francisco: Washington Research Institute, June 1985]. The above quote appears on p. 52.)

15. Fera, "The Day After," p. 13.

16. "Bhopal: What Really Happened?," *Business India*, p. 115; Fera, "The Day After," pp. 12, 13. *Business India* reports that Dr. Chandra was told by Dr. Misra, "You are a doctor of the dead, so do not interfere with the living."

17. "Bhopal: What Really Happened?," *Business India*, p. 115.

18. Cited in ibid. *Business India* reports that Dr. Daunderer was "bundled out of Bhopal."
19. Dr. Chandra, interview with author.
20. OSHA, "Occupational Health Guideline for Methyl Isocyanate," September 1978, p. 2.
21. "Carbide Misleads on MIC," *Madhya Pradesh Chronicle* (Bhopal), 26 March 1985. The *Chronicle* reports that Carbide confidential manual number UC 4744376 states on page 2 that MIC can decompose at 218° C., and that Carbide booklet F-414431/76 No. 17 states, "'Thermal decomposition may produce hydrogen cyanide, nitrogen oxide, carbon monoxide . . ." (in Pinto and O'Leary, *Reprints on Union Carbide Chemical Incident*, p. 65).

    Madhya Pradesh Department of the Environment took six air samples on 5 December and reported that two of them, taken near the MIC tanks, were positive for cyanide ("Bhopal: What Really Happened?," *Business India*, p. 116).
22. Dr. N. P. Misra, interview with author, 20 February 1985, Bhopal. (All subsequent quotes by Dr. Misra are from this interview unless otherwise stated.)
23. F. William Sunderman and F. William Sunderman Jr., eds., *Laboratory Diagnosis of Diseases Caused by Toxic Agents* (London: Adam Hilger; St. Louis: Warren H. Green, Inc., 1970), p. 289.
24. Dr. B. B. L. Mathur, interview with author, 21 February 1985, Bhopal. (All subsequent quotes by Dr. Mathur are from this interview unless otherwise stated.)
25. ICMR, "Minutes of the Meeting on Thiosulphate Therapy in MIC Exposed Population Held on 14 February 1985 at ICMR Headquarters, New Delhi," in Pinto and O'Leary, *Reprints on Union Carbide Chemical Incident*, p. 41.

    In late February 1985, one Dr. A. S. Paintal tried to further muddy the waters by stating at a conference in New Delhi that he didn't know whether "the victims had died of the methyl isocyanate or sodium thiosulphate," a statement Dr. Chandra labeled "incorrect, irresponsible, and antinational" ("'Wrong' Drug Used in Bhopal," *Hindustan Times*, 24 February 1985; "Bhopal Gas Antidote Controversy Hots Up," *Hindustan Times* [New Delhi], 25 February 1985).
26. Dr. S. Sriramachari, interview with author, 14 March 1985, New Delhi. One family I visited who lived in a hut just east of Union Carbide had medicines galore, including a bottle, five plastic packets, and several paper pouches containing at least 100 pills of various sorts; electral powder for dehydration, and bottles of glaxo antacid, cough medicine, and chest rub. Their four-year-old girl was playing with empty vials labeled streptomycin sulphate. This family had never heard of sodium thiosulphate.
27. ICMR, "Medical Research on Bhopal Gas Tragedy" (press release, New Delhi), 12 February 1985. Elevated thiocyanate levels from Dr.

Ishwar Das, additional chief secretary in charge of co-ordinating health and relief services for the state of Madhya Pradesh, interview with author, 26 February 1985, Bhopal.

28. ICMR, "ICMR Guidelines for Treatment of Bhopal Gas Victims" (press release), 4 April 1985 (reproduced in Pinto and O'Leary, *Reprints on Union Carbide Chemical Incident*).

29. Author's interview with doctors at the thirty-bed clinic, 28 February 1985, Bhopal.

30. In a 31 January press release, the Madhya Pradesh government stated, "Sodium-thiosulphate is available for administration to the patients and for scientific studies on its effects on the MIC affected patients. No instructions have been issued by government not to administer sodium thiosulphate. It is only indicated if there is evidence of cyanide toxicity in the body as a result of MIC" (Directorate of Information and Publicity, MP State Government, "Intensive Health Care of Gas Victims – Medical Efforts Get Momentum" (press release), 31 January 1985).

31. Dr. Misra also argues that sodium thiosulphate treatment would not have saved lives because those exposed to cyanide died immediately. Yet according to records at Gandhi Medical College, 250 people died at Hamidia Hospital on 4 December, and another 170 died by the end of the month.

At a 24 March conference in Bhopal, Dr. Misra reportedly argued that the culprit in the 2–3 December catastrophe was carbon monoxide, not cyanide, because it too can leave victims with cherry-red venous blood. However, Dr. Chandra argued that carbon monoxide poisoning was impossible in an open space, since it rises above denser atmospheric gases, and because carbon monoxide poisoning would be marked by an inability of the blood to coagulate, something not found in Bhopal victims (cited in Susanna Dakin, "Bhopal: A Personal View," in Pinto and O'Leary, *Reprints on Union Carbide Chemical Incident*, p. 10). In addition, Dr. Sriramachari said that ICMR tests of carboxy hemoglobin (carbon monoxide) levels in the blood of gas victims were negative (interview with author).

32. Dr. Abhay Bang et al. (Medico Friends Circle), "Medical Relief and Research in Bhopal – The Realities and Recommendations" (mimeographed report presented to the All-India Convention of Peoples' Science, Democratic Rights and Environmental Protection Groups called by the Zahreeli Gas Kand Sangharsh Morcha, Bhopal, 17 and 18 February, 1985), p. 1. (This document is available in Pinto and O'Leary, *Reprints on Union Carbide Chemical Incident*.)

33. See "Give Sodium Thiosulphate – Women Stage Angry Demonstration," *The Hitavada* (Bhopal), 25 March 1985, in Pinto and O'Leary, *Reprints on Union Carbide Chemical Incident*, p. 66.

34. Susanna Dakin, "Bhopal: A Personal View," in Pinto and O'Leary, *Reprints on Union Carbide Chemical Incident*, p. 7.

35. "MP Panel Condemns Doctors' Harassment," *Indian Express* (New Delhi), 27 June 1985. The charges against the clinic are from Talmiz Ahmad, interview with author.
36. The UCC doctors were Dr. Hilton Lewison, assistant corporate medical director, and Dr. Bryan Ballantyne, corporate director of applied toxicology (Directorate of Information and Publicity, Government of Madhya Pradesh, "Dr. Ishwar Das Asks Union Carbide for Information" [mimeographed press release], 27 February 1985). Dr. Ballantyne was formerly a senior medical officer (research) for the British Ministry of Defense at the Chemical Defense Establishment at Porton Down, England, and is an expert in cyanide poisoning (see Bryan Ballantyne, ed., *Forensic Toxicology* [Bristol, England: John Wright and Sons Limited, 1974]).
37. UCC, "Union Carbide Establishes Programs to Study Toxicological Effects of Overexposure to Methyl Isocyanate" (press release), 15 March 1985.
38. Cited in "New Bhopal Dispute: Cyanide Poisoning of Victims Claimed," *C&EN*, 22 July 1985, p. 6.
39. UCC, "Bhopal Incident Report," especially p. 24. UCC did not respond to a question by the author concerning what the company knew of the chemicals that escaped from tank 610.
40. "For Bhopal Survivors, Recovery is Agonizing, Illnesses are Insidious," *Wall Street Journal*, 1 April 1985.
41. "Doctors in India Disagree on Drug," *New York Times*, 10 April 1985.
42. "Bhopal Report – Data on MIC's Toxicity are Scant, Leave Much to be Learned," *C&EN*, 11 February 1985, p. 39. In July 1985, *C&EN* carried another article on the cyanide controversy, cited above in n. 38.
43. Ronald Wishart before House Subcommittee on Asian and Pacific Affairs, "Implications of Bhopal Disaster," p. 32.
44. Dr. N. R. Bhandari, superintendent of Hamidia Hospital, said Indian medical authorities had been consulting with UCC on treating the victims immediately after the disaster ("As Death Toll Climbs, India Now Fears Epidemic," *New York Times*, 6 December 1984).
    While it is beyond the scope of this book to examine the World Health Organization and its role in Bhopal, it should be noted that Dr. K. W. Jager, a doctor from WHO, came to Bhopal in early December 1984, shortly after the disaster, and also rejected the cyanide diagnosis and sodium thiosulphate treatment, arguing that the symptomatic line of treatment was correct (Fera, "The Day After," p. 13). On 11 December he also stated that there was little likelihood of paralysis or kidney or liver complications from the gas exposure, and no basis for fear that pregnant women or fetuses would suffer abnormally ("Paralysis Among Gas Victims Ruled Out," *Hindustan Times*, 11 December 1984).
    For more on the cyanide poisoning in Bhopal, see "Signs of Cyanide Poisoning," *Times of India* (Bombay), 26 March 1985; "Car-

bide Lobby Hampers Victims' Treatment," *Indian Express* (New Delhi), 27 March 1985. Both of these articles are reprinted in Pinto and O'Leary, *Reprints on Union Carbide Chemical Incident.*

45. Arun Subramaniam of *Business India,* speaking at the conference "After Bhopal – Implications for Developed and Developing Nations," Newark, N.J., 20–21 March 1985.

46. ICFTU, "Trade Union Report," p. 13.

47. Zahreeli Gas Kand Sangharsh Morcha, "Partial Survey – Jayprakash Nagar, Nichala Chhola, and Assorted Bastis" (handwritten summary of results provided by Dr. Anil Sadgopal), 3 January 1985.

48. Dr. S. R. Kamat, interview with author, 9 March 1985, Bombay. (All subsequent comments by Dr. Kamat are from this interview unless otherwise stated.)

49. Figure of 65,000 living in most affected areas provided by Dr. S. N. Sharma, Department of Preventative Medicine, Gandhi Medical College, Bhopal, interview with author, 21 February 1985.

50. "Bhopal Casualty Figures Challenged – Carbide Lawyer Says Numbers Significantly Exaggerated," *Washington Post,* 18 April 1985, sec. B.

51. UCC, "Proposed Industrial Hygiene Monitoring Program for 1984," 28 November 1983 (cited in House Subcommittee on Health and the Environment, "Hazardous Air Pollutants," pp. 523–33).

52. UCC, "Union Carbide Physician Praises Indian Medical Response" (press release), 21 December 1984, p. 2.

53. See UCC press statement cited in n. 14.

54. Cited in "Effects of Gas Uncertain," *Statesman* (New Delhi), 16 December 1984; "Dr. Halberg Admits Total Blindness Cases in Bhopal," *The Hitavada,* 15 December 1984.

55. Cited in "Dr. Halberg Admits Total Blindness Cases in Bhopal," *The Hitavada.*

56. Indian government estimate of irreparable damage from Talmiz Ahmad, telephone interview with author, 13 August 1985, New York.

57. Cited in "Carbide Misled Doctors," *Indian Express,* in Pinto and O'Leary, *Reprints on Union Carbide Chemical Incident,* p. 62.

58. Morcha, "Partial Survey."

59. Bang et al., "Medical Relief and Research in Bhopal," p. 2.

60. "Six Deformed Babies in India Linked to Bhopal Gas Leak," *New York Times,* 16 July 1985. A 16 July 1985 article in the *Times of India* (Bombay) says it was not six, but twenty-one babies who were born deformed.

61. Cited in "Worst is Far from Over in Bhopal," *Times of India,* 23 January 1985.

62. Bang et al., "Medical Relief and Research in Bhopal," p. 2.

63. Dr. Sharma Narain, interview with author, 18 February 1985, Bhopal.

64. Dr. Rani Bang, "Effects of the Bhopal Disaster on the Women's

Health – An Epidemic of Gynecological Diseases" (study done between 27 February and 15 March 1985), in Pinto and O'Leary,
Reprints on Union Carbide Chemical Incident, pp. 35–37.

65. Dr. Paul Shrivastava, telephone interview with author, 8 August
1985, New York.
66. "Carbide Buys Up Bhopal Doctors," *Indian Express* (Bangalore),
21 June 1985.
67. "Could It Happen in America?," *Newsweek,* 17 December 1984, p. 20.
There have been few animal studies on the effects of MIC, and fewer
still on humans. The British medical journal *Lancet* reports that no
work on MIC was recorded in its index for the past seven years ("Carbide Misled Doctors," *Indian Express* [Bombay], 28 January 1985, in
Pinto and O'Leary, *Reprints on Union Carbide Chemical Incident,* p. 62).
One doctor stated that there had been few studies on MIC because it
was so toxic and volatile ("Health Crisis Could Last Years, Experts
Say," *New York Times,* 7 December 1984).
The ICMR is planning some fifteen different studies on the effects of MIC and the other chemicals involved in the disasters on the
gas-affected.
68. Dr. Das, interview with author.
69. "Data on MIC's Toxicity Scant," *C&EN,* p. 37.
70. Van Den Ameele, UCC press spokesperson, telephone interview with
author, 8 August 1985.
71. Cited in "Bhopal Casualty Figures Challenged," *Washington Post.*
72. "Disabling and Incurable Ailments Still Afflict Thousands in Bhopal,"
New York Times, 29 March 1985; "For Bhopal Survivors, Recovery is
Agonizing, Illnesses are Insidious," *Wall Street Journal,* 1 April 1985.
73. "Warren Anderson: A Public Crisis, A Personal Ordeal," *New York
Times,* 19 May 1985, sec. 3.
74. Dr. Abhay Bang, interview with author, 18 February 1985, Bhopal.
75. "Treating Bhopal Victims," *Indian Express* (Bombay), 31 January 1985.

5 | Reaping the Benefits

1. "The Bhopal Tragedy," *Wall Street Journal,* 10 December 1985.
2. UCC, "Concluding Remarks – Warren M. Anderson," p. 4.
3. Cited in "The Bhopal Tragedy," *Wall Street Journal.*
4. All statistics from CMIE, *Basic Statistics, 1983,* "Table 12.12-1," except
number of tractors from Bharat Dogra, *Poverty, Development and
Poverty: India 1947–84* (New Delhi: Bharat Dogra, 1984), p. 180.
5. "India 1984: The Pattern of Mis-Development," *Business India,* 14–27
January 1985, p. 116.

6. Indian statistics from CMIE, *Basic Statistics, 1983,* "Table 2.2: Trends in Death Rates, Infant Mortality and Expectation of Life"; U.S. statistics from *Information Please Almanac 1985,* pp. 777, 781.

7. Susan George, *How the Other Half Dies: The Real Reasons for World Hunger* (Totowa, New Jersey: Rowman & Allanheld, 1977), p. 99.

8. Frances Moore Lappe and Joseph Collins, *Food First: Beyond the Myth of Scarcity* (New York: Ballantine, 1979), p. 174.

9. George, *How the Other Half Dies,* p. 102.

10. Lappe and Collins, *Food First,* pp. 140, 141. They also note, "In the Indian Punjab, between the fifties and the mid-sixties, the amount of land owned by the largest farmers (those with 100–150 acres) increased at a rate four to ten times greater than that of the smaller-sized farmer" (p. 139).

11. Ibid., p. 136.

12. Centre for Science and Environment (CSE), *The State of India's Environment 1982: A Citizen's Report* (New Delhi: Centre for Science and Environment, 1982), p. 92.

13. Dogra, *Poverty, Development and Poverty,* p. 12.

14. CSE, *State of Environment,* pp. 92, 130, 138–39, 126.

15. CMIE, *Basic Statistics, 1983,* "Table 13.1."

16. CMIE, *Basic Statistics, 1983,* "Table 2.2: Trends in Death Rates, Infant Mortality and Expectation of Life."

17. CSE, *State of Environment,* p. 92.

18. Dogra, *Poverty, Development and Poverty,* pp. 4–5. Lappe and Collins note that cropland planted in legumes, which have two to four times the protein content of grain, has declined by 2.5 million acres, and between 1965 and 1971 the average daily consumption of legumes in India declined by 31 percent (Lappe and Collins, *Food First,* p. 153).

19. Dogra, *Poverty, Development and Poverty,* pp. 5, 3.

20. Cited in "India 1984: The Pattern of Mis-Development," *Business India,* p. 117.

21. UCIL, *Annual Report 1983,* p. 3.

22. Lappe and Collins, *Food First,* p. 167.

23. David Weir and Mark Shapiro, *Circle of Poison* (San Francisco: Institute for Food and Development Policy, 1981), p. 32.

24. UCIL, *Annual Report 1983,* p. 10; UCIL, *Annual Report 1980,* p. 8. For a discussion of the impact of commercial fishing on India's fisherfolk, see Ramakrishnan Korakandy, "Purse Sein Fishing in Kerala: Its Economics and Politics," in *E&PW,* 31 March 1984; and CSE, *State of Environment,* p. 113. Dogra writes, "Similarly the fisheries sector has become more and more integrated in the international market in recent years. While consumption of fish by the poor people of coastal areas is declining, the export of fishmeal at cheap prices to feed the poultry and cats of developed countries has increased" (Dogra, *Poverty, Development and Poverty,* p. 211).

25. CMIE, *Basic Statistics, 1983,* "Table 12.12: Last, An Overall View of

Recent Trends in Agricultural Inputs – 1966-67 to 1983-84," emphasis in original.

26. Ibid.
27. "India 1984: The Pattern of Mis-Development," *Business India*, 14–27 January 1985, p. 117.
28. Dogra, *Poverty, Development and Poverty*, p. 179. Dogra also adds that in Punjab, loans from primary agricultural credit societies are twice as high, per hectare cropped, as the all-India average (p. 171).
29. Ibid., p. 179.
30. "Hazards from Pesticides – II: The Most Dreaded Phenomenon," *Times of India*, second article in series appearing from 15 to 18 December 1982. Dogra notes, "Long term impediment of the fertility of land, alarming deficiency in micro-nutrients, increased threat from pests and diseases, severe waterlogging and salinity problems in canal irrigated areas, outbreak of water borne diseases and the increased exposure of workers to occupational health hazards – these are some of the environmental problems brought or accentuated by the green revolution" (Dogra, *Poverty, Development and Poverty*, p. 188).
31. CSE, *State of Environment*, pp. 134-37.
32. David Weir, "Global Pesticide Issues," ICCR (Interfaith Center on Corporate Responsibility) Brief Vol. 13, No. 3, 1984 (New York: ICCR, 1984), p. 3A.
33. "Gassed," *The Week* (New Delhi), 16–22 December 1984, p. 24.
34. Dogra, *Poverty, Development and Poverty*, pp. 184-88. Dogra notes, "In recent years the Indian government has been giving a massive subsidy on the import of nitrogenous fertilisers." See also George, *How the Other Half Dies*, pp. 90-93.
35. CMIE, *Basic Statistics, 1983*, "Table 20.1: Imports, Exports and Trade Balance – 1938-39 and 1948-49 to 1983-84."
36. Dogra, *Poverty, Development and Poverty*, p. 184.
37. George, *How the Other Half Dies*, p. 93.
38. Raymond Lotta with Frank Shannon, *America in Decline: An Analysis of the Developments Toward War and Revolution, in the U.S. and Worldwide, in the 1980s* (Chicago: Banner Press, 1984), pp. 103-104. Statistic on world hunger from transcript of television program *Hunger for Profit* (New York: Robert Richter Productions, 1984), p. 1.
39. Lappe and Collins, *Food First*, p. 16.
40. *Hunger for Profit* (television program transcript), p. 5.

6 | India's Complicity and Dependence

1. See, for example, "Preventing Future Bhopals," *Business Week*,

24 December 1984, p. 90; "Plant Had to be Locally Designed and Operated," *New York Times,* 13 December 1984; "Gas Leak is Expected to Reduce Investment in Third World," *New York Times,* 12 December 1984; Macdonald, "Affidavit in Support of Union Carbide"; "Workers at Site of Leak Described as Unskilled," *New York Times,* 6 December 1984.

2. Gladwin and Walter, "Bhopal and the Multinational," *Wall Street Journal.*
3. CMIE, *Basic Statistics Relating to the Indian Economy, Vol. 1: All India, August 1984* (Bombay: CMIE, 1984), "Table 22.12: Foreign Collaborations Approved by Government of India – 1948 to 1984."
4. Stockholm International Peace Research Institute, "Arms Trade with the Third World," (Stockholm, 1971), p. 753, cited in Santosh K. Mehrotra and Patrick Clawson, "Soviet Economic Relations with India and Other Third World Countries," in Editors of The Communist, eds., *The Soviet Union: Socialist or Social-Imperialist?–Essays Toward the Debate on the Nature of Soviet Society* (Chicago: RCP Publications, 1983), p. 128. (Mehrotra and Clawson's essay is reprinted from *E&PW,* Special Number August 1979.)
5. CMIE, *Basic Statistics, 1984,* "Table 22.5-1: Sources of External Assistance and Outstanding Debt."
6. George, *How the Other Half Dies,* p. 92.
7. Dogra, *Poverty, Development and Poverty,* p. 255.
8. See Mehrotra and Clawson, "Soviet Economic Relations with India," pp. 98-108.
9. CMIE, *Basic Statistics, 1983,* "Table 20.4: Major Trading Partners of India – 1970-71 and 1980-81."
10. Dogra, *Poverty, Development and Poverty,* p. 259. See also Mehrotra and Clawson, "Soviet Economic Relations with India" pp. 103-114. According to the *Economic Times* (Bombay) of 18 February 1984, "India is being virtually compelled to increase its purchases from the Soviet Union this year, even if this means reduction in freight rates to make certain Russian items competitive vis-a-vis supplies from other countries" (cited in Dogra, p. 260).
11. "From Independence to Indira Gandhi," *Fortune India,* pp. 4-5.
12. CMIE, *Basic Statistics, 1983,* "Table 20.1: Imports, Exports and Trade Balance – 1938-39 and 1948-49 to 1983-84."
13. CMIE, *Basic Statistics, 1984,* "Table 22.6: External Debt of India"; "Table 22.4: Inflow of External Assistance, Gross and Net"; and "Table 22.3: Inflow of Foreign Assistance – 1961-62 to 1984-85."
14. Dogra, *Poverty, Development and Poverty,* p. 259.
15. "Red Carpet for Foreign Capital," *E&PW,* 23 February 1985, pp. 311-12. In 1980, 434 branches and 125 subsidiaries of foreign companies had assets of approximately $3.16 billion in India ("Profitability of Foreign Companies in India," *Indo-U.S. Chamber of Commerce Newsletter* (New Delhi), September 1980, p. 13), and ac-

counted for 18 percent of the total value added in mining and manufacturing in the private corporate sector (CMIE, *Basic Statistics, 1984,* "Table 22.11: Foreign Investment Approved by the Government of India – 1978 to 1983"). CMIE criticizes those who "talk in highly emotional and exaggerated terms about exploitation of India by foreign-based Multi National Corporations (MNCs) operating in India" (ibid.), and cites the 18 percent figure as proof that foreign capital doesn't dominate the Indian economy. However, the absolute percentage of foreign ownership is less important than the fact that it is concentrated in the key leading sectors of the Indian economy. Over 55 percent of foreign investment is in manufacturing industries, of which 21 percent is in the chemical industry (CMIE, *Basic Statistics, 1984,* "Table 22.10: Foreign Private Investment in India, Cumulative Total – 1948 to 1974").

16. "New Turn to Row Over Carbide Site," *Times of India,* 13 February 1985.
17. "Curbs Give Way to Welcome for Multinational Companies," *New York Times,* 11 May 1985.
18. Macdonald, "Affidavit in Support of Union Carbide," pp. 1, 4.
19. UCIL, *Annual Report 1983,* p. 44.
20. S. Kumaraswami, interview with author, 13 March 1985, New Delhi (all subsequent quotes from this interview unless otherwise stated).
21. "Profitability of Foreign Companies in India," *Indo-U.S. Chamber of Commerce Newsletter,* p. 13.
22. Cited in "Gas Leak Expected to Reduce Investment," *New York Times.*
23. S. Kumaraswami, interview with author.
24. Macdonald, "Affidavit in Support of Union Carbide," p. 4.
25. UCIL, *Annual Report 1983,* p. 25.
26. Cited in Dogra, *Poverty, Development and Poverty,* p. 263. The Indo-U.S. Chamber of Commerce reported that "The business climate in India for foreign investors has considerably improved over the past few years and doing business with India – despite difficulties in the past – can now be both pleasant and profitable" ("Doing Business with India," *Indo-U.S. Chamber of Commerce Newsletter,* September 1981, p. 11).
27. The Water Pollution Control Act was passed in 1974 and the Prevention and Control of Air Pollution Act in 1981. Previously, industrial production was regulated by the Factories Act of 1948 and, in the case of pesticides, by the Pesticides Act of 1968.
28. "Danger Zone – Chemical-Plant Safety is Still Just Developing in Developing Nations," *Wall Street Journal.*
29. S. Kumaraswami, interview with author.
30. "Did Buch Okay Carbide Plant Site?," *Hindustan Times* (New Delhi), 13 February 1985.
31. "New Turn to Row Over Carbide Site," *Times of India.*
32. Only within the past two years have new government regulations for-

bidden new or expanded industrial activity in cities of over one-half million people; and it wasn't until June 1984, six months before the catastrophe in Bhopal, that the Ministry of Industry in New Delhi stipulated that industrial licenses shouldn't be granted without environmental clearances ("Where Does the Blame Lie?," *New York Times*).

33. Department of Town and Country Planning, *Bhopal Development Plan*, pp. 225–28.
34. Directorate of Economics and Statistics, "Salient Facts of Madhya Pradesh," pp. 13, 14.
35. M. N. Buch, interview with author, 2 March 1985, Bhopal.
36. Department of Town and Country Planning, *Bhopal Development Plan*, p. 159.
37. Cited in "Industrial Safety – Belated Awakening," *India Today*, 31 January 1985, p. 63. *India Today* reports that the maximum fine for violating safety standards is only 2,000 rupees ($154) or three months imprisonment (p. 62).
38. "Where Does Blame Lie," *New York Times*. (The figure of 286 inspections is from "Belated Awakening," *India Today*, pp. 62–63.) *India Today* states that "At least half the 11,200 factories in [the state of] Karnataka were not inspected for safety by state factory inspectors last year" (p. 63).
39. Dr. A. N. Verma, principal secretary of Department of Environment, Government of Madhya Pradesh; interview with author, 26 February 1985, Bhopal. (All subsequent quotes by Dr. Verma are from this interview unless otherwise stated.)
40. "Where Does Blame Lie," *New York Times*.
41. B. P. Srivastava, interview with author.
42. Ravi Shevade, interview with author, 18 February 1985, Bhopal. This attitude was quite evident in talking to government officials responsible for environmental regulation. "It is not the general practice" to allow industry to police itself, stated Dr. G. K. Khare, second in command at the pollution control board, but "it should have been solely the management's responsibility to warn the workers and community" (interview with author, 22 February 1985, Bhopal). "Ultimately you always come back to the management," Dr. Verma insisted. And chief minister Arjun Singh said, "Union Carbide did not inform the government or the municipal authorities here about the inherent hazards in the manufacture of this commodity . . . at no point in time did Union Carbide on their own even suggest that there could be this dimension of damage from any of the ingredients that they were using in their manufacturing process" (interview with author, 3 March 1985, Bhopal).
43. Zariwala stated, "When workers complained [about safety], the inspectors would come to the factory, see the officials, look around, and then go away."

44. Government of Madhya Pradesh, "Accidents in Union Carbide," pp. 1–2. The situation was no better in terms of water pollution. The toxicity of the chemicals used at the Carbide plant was dramatically illustrated when, several years before the 2–3 December catastrophe, cattle died after drinking from effluent ponds on company grounds. Subsequently the ponds were monitored by the pollution control board, but no questions were asked about what sorts of chemicals caused these deaths, or what the broader dangers of their use were. "Since there was no effluent going out of the premises of the factory, what was inside the tanks does not become a subject for our investigation," said Dr. Verma.

45. "Carbide's Lapses Ignored," *Times of India* (Bombay), 3 January 1985.

46. Following the appearance of his articles, Keswani was visited by unidentified goons (Raajkumar Keswani, interview with author, 24 February 1985, Bhopal).

47. Quotes in this and the preceding paragraph cited in "Government's False Promises," *Free Press Journal*, 16 December 1984.

48. "Many Pesticide Units Evade Safety Rules," *Hindustan Times*, 13 December 1984.

49. "Industry vs. Safety," *Update* (Bombay), 6–19 February 1985, p. 21.

50. The Factories Act of 1948 mandates that plants with over 1,000 employees using hazardous processes must establish safety offices. In the state of Maharashtra only 97 out of 224 such units have done so. In West Bengal the figure is 35 out of 183; in Andhra Pradesh, 27 out of 80 ("The Grim Wages of Neglect," *Business World* (Calcutta), 18 February–3 March 1985, p. 83).

51. CSE, *State of Environment*, pp. 16, 72.

52. V. T. Padmanabhan, *The Gas Chamber on the Chambal* (New Delhi: People's Union for Civil Liberties, 1983), p. 51, 31.

53. "The Grim Wages of Neglect," *Business World*, p. 68.

54. "How Hazardous Are Our Workplaces?," *Industrial Times*, 7–20 January 1985, p. 36.

55. "Industry vs. Safety," *Update*, pp. 18–19.

56. "Death in Bhopal: Compensation Seems Not Quite the Point," *Wall Street Journal*. The *Journal* reported that India's Department of Environment found four times the U.S. lead limit in Indian battery plants, six times the sulfur dioxide limit in chemical plants, and seven times the ammonia limit in fertilizer plants. UCIL is the largest manufacturer of batteries in India.

57. Macdonald, "Affidavit in Support of Union Carbide," p. 5.

58. It is also ironic to hear such charges in light of the EPA's record of "regulating" the U.S. chemical industry. In the fifteen years it has had the authority to regulate factory emissions, the EPA has set standards on precisely eight chemicals. Eight years ago the EPA put thirty-seven chemicals on a priority study list; today they are still not regulated. Of the 20,000-plus toxic chemical dumps in the U.S. today,

there are 812 on the EPA "national priority list"; ten have been completely cleaned up in five years. ("Toxic Air and the EPA Tortoise," *New York Times*, 17 June 1985; "Toxic Waste Concentration Spurs Extra Effort," *New York Times*, 28 April 1985; "Mired in the Superfund Swamp," *New York Times*, 5 August 1985.)
59. "A Three Mile Island for Chemicals," *New York Times*, 16 December 1984.
60. Prepared statement of Robert A. Peck, deputy assistant secretary, Bureau of Near Eastern and South Asian Affairs, Department of State, in House Subcommittee on Asian and Pacific Affairs, "Implications of Bhopal Disaster," p. 13.
61. G.A.O. Report No. CED-79-43, 22 June 1979, cited in Weir, "Global Pesticide Issues," p. 3A.
62. Weir, "Global Pesticide Issues," p. 3B.
63. David Bull, *A Growing Problem: Pesticides and the Third World Poor* (Oxford: Oxfam, 1982), pp. 37–38.
64. "Poisoning on Wide Scale," *Times of India*, 15 December 1982.
65. Speth, in House Subcommittee on Asian and Pacific Affairs, "Implications of Bhopal Disaster," p. 48.
66. Bob Wyrick, "World Suffers Side Effects of U.S.-Made Drugs," *Newsday*, 15 December 1981.
67. Barry I. Castleman, "The Double Standard in Industrial Hazards," in *Multinational Monitor*, September 1984, pp. 4–6; and Castleman, "The Double Standard in Industrial Hazards," *International Journal of Health Services*, Vol. 13, No. 1, p. 9.
68. Bob Wyrick, "How Job Conditions Led to a Worker's Death," *Newsday*, 17 December 1981. Wyrick writes, "The Union Carbide operation in Indonesia exemplifies a situation that *Newsday* found again and again during its year-long examination of U.S.-based corporations' activities in developing nations."
69. "A Three Mile Island for Chemicals," *New York Times*.

7 | In the Horror's Aftermath

1. UCC, "Opening Remarks – Warren M. Anderson," pp. 1–2.
2. Cited in "Carbide Faults Workers in India," *The Record* (Hackensack, NJ), 21 March 1985.
3. Van Den Ameele, telephone interview with author.
4. Cited in "Accord on Interim Aid to Bhopal Seen Near," *New York Times*, 8 August 1985.
5. Kelley Drye & Warren, "Memorandum in Support of Union Carbide," p. 5.

6. UCIL officials, interview with author, 16 March 1985, Bombay.

7. UCC, "Van Mynen Presentation," p. 12.

8. First it should be noted that Union Carbide itself admits its investigation has been hampered by many limitations and that it has no proof of sabotage. The company was only able to talk to the works manager and the MIC production manager, who weren't on duty the night of the disaster, and had "informal" conversations with a "few witnesses to the event." (UCC, "Van Mynen Presentation," p. 3; "Bhopal Incident Report," p. i.) In India, Gokhale admitted that Union Carbide had not been able to examine the pipelines to determine how the water went into tank 610.

   Reporters for *Business India* and the *Times of India,* Ravi Shevade, a chemical engineer from Bombay, as well as the delegation from the International Federation of Chemical, Energy and General Workers' Unions all interviewed most of the workers involved in the incident and found no evidence to support the sabotage hypothesis. The ICFTU "Trade Union Report" states that sabotage can be "ruled out" and that "there was never any evidence for such an act" (p. 12). Workers supportive of the Morcha also denied the accident had been the result of sabotage. When first interviewed on the morning of the disaster, works manager Mukund ruled out the possibility of sabotage. " 'Our men are really good,' he said. Moreover, why would anybody do it, he asked" ("Top Safety Steps Claimed," *Free Press Journal,* 4 December 1984, p. 1).

   It would have been difficult for a worker to accidentally introduce water into the MIC tanks from the nearby utility station. As the "Trade Union Report" points out, "Nor is it clear why someone would wish to hook up a nitrogen line from the utility station to tank 610, since nitrogen can easily be introduced into the tank through permanent fixed lines" (p. 7). A former engineer at the plant told the *New York Times* that it would also have been difficult to connect a water line to the nitrogen nozzle inadvertently because the lines have nozzles of different sizes and are labeled and color-coded: nitrogen gray, air lines white, and water lines blue ("Union Carbide's Inquiry Indicates Errors Led to India Plant Disaster," *New York Times,* 21 March 1985).

9. UCC, "Bhopal Incident Report," p. 21.

10. "The Cover-Up," *Sunday.*

11. "Labor Report on Bhopal Cites Plant Modification," *New York Times.*

12. "The exact source of the water is not known, but laboratory work demonstrated that 1,000 to 2,000 pounds of water would have accounted for the chemistry of the residue" (UCC, "Bhopal Incident Report," p. 21).

13. Dr. Srinivasan Varadarajan, the head of the Indian government's Council for Scientific and Industrial Research, interview with author, 15 March 1985, New Delhi. Arun Subramaniam of *Business India*

estimates that between 150 and 200 liters of water entered tank 610.

14. Talmiz Ahmad, phone interview with author. UCC's press spokesman claimed that there were posters "all over the place" (telephone interview, September 1985).

15. Union of Soviet Socialist Republic's Mission to the United Nations, "Review of Soviet Press – India" (press release, number 21), 26–28 January 1985.

16. "NATO Generals Visited Carbide?," *Madhya Pradesh Chronicle,* 21 February 1985. The secretary of the CPI also said that two NATO generals had visited the Carbide factory in the garb of scientists before the disaster, implying that the disaster had been a deliberate experiment in chemical warfare.

17. "UCC Catering to NATO for Chemical Warfare," *Indian Express,* 11 February 1985, p. 11.

18. "Leak Part of U.S. Gas Warfare," *The Daily,* 21 January 1985, p. 9.

19. See also "Carbide, Pentagon Colluded in Conducting Secret Experiments," *The Patriot,* 29 December 1984, p. 8; "The Guinea-Pig Controversy," *Now,* January 1985, pp. 42–51; Delhi Science Forum, "Bhopal Gas Tragedy – Delhi Science Forum Report" (New Delhi: Society for Delhi Science Forum, n.d.).

   UCC denials from B. P. Srivastava, interview with author; Van Den Ameele, telephone interview with author. The U.S. Army Media Relations Office states that UCC presently has no contracts with the Department of Defense for the production of or for research and development in chemical and/or biological weapons. However, UCC does have a contract for investigating the most effective way to transport such weapons – specifically shells. The Army says the purpose of this study is to determine the best way to transport shells so they can be destroyed. UCC is not one of the top 500 defense contractors and in 1984 had slightly over $2 million in defense contracts (Lt. Col. Craig McNabb, U.S. Army Media Relations, telephone interview with author, 13 August 1985).

20. Manhattan project: "Calamity for Union Carbide," *Time,* 17 December 1984, p. 38. Y-12: Van Den Ameele, telephone interview; UCC, "Notice of Annual Meeting of Stockholders to be held on April 27, 1983," 21 March 1983, pp. 26–27.

21. Ronald Reagan, cited in "India Seizes Executives in Gas Leak," *Philadelphia Inquirer,* 7 December 1984.

22. Peck, in House Subcommittee on Asian and Pacific Affairs, "Implications of Bhopal Disaster," pp. 1, 11–12.

23. Ibid., pp. 11–12.

24. Public relations officer, Near East–South Asian Affairs, Department of State, telephone interview with author, 13 August 1985.

25. See "Reagan Hails Plan on Tax and Hints Cuts for Military," and "Transcript of News Conference with President," *New York Times,* 8 December 1984.

26. "U.S. Lone Dissenter in U.N. Vote on Listing of Restricted Products," *New York Times*, 19 December 1984.

27. Peck, in House Subcommittee on Asian and Pacific Affairs, "Implications of Bhopal Disaster," pp. 13-14.

28. See "Hazardous Air Pollutants"; "Industry Chiefs Back U.S. Curbs on Polluted Air," *New York Times*, 27 March 1985, p. 1; "India Tragedy Prompts Chemical Firms, Public Authorities to Review Safety Steps," *Wall Street Journal*, 7 December 1985, p. 2; "Carbide Suits May Affect Industry Norms," *Wall Street Journal*, 5 April 1985, p. 6. One executive told the *New York Times* that one reason the chemical industry was now supporting legislation was that after Bhopal the public "simply does not have faith that the chemical industry will regulate itself in the public interest" ("Industry Chiefs Back Curbs," *New York Times*). The only concrete step taken by the Administration was an agreement between the U.S. Agency for International Development and a number of U.S. multinationals to help developing countries "prevent and respond to industrial accidents." The plan called for U.S. "industrial experts" to be dispatched to factories in developing countries "to work closely with local plant managers in creating systems to meet emergency needs" (United States Information Service, "U.S.A.I.D. Announces Safety Program in Response to Bhopal Tragedy" [press release], American Center, New Delhi, 31 January 1985).

29. Cited in "Chemical Safety in Developing Countries," *C&EN*, p. 10.

30. "Preventing Future Bhopals," *Business Week*, p. 90.

31. "I.B.M. Concessions to Mexico," *New York Times*, 25 July 1985.

32. "Bhopal: A *C&EN* Special Issue," *C&EN*, 11 February 1985, p. 14. "The children do not understand what happened to them and their families that dreadful night," *C&EN* writes. "Their parents don't really comprehend it either."

33. Cited in "India Seizes Executives in Gas Leak," *Philadelphia Inquirer.*

34. United States Information Service, "Sorting Out Bhopal Disaster Will Take Time, Bajpai Says," (USIS Backgrounder), American Center, New Delhi; 12 December 1984.

35. Cited in "India Seizes Executives in Gas Leak," *Philadelphia Inquirer.*

36. "Gandhi Solicits Foreign Investment in India," *Washington Post*, 16 April 1985.

37. "Red Carpet for Foreign Capital," *E&PW*, 23 February 1985, p. 311.

38. "Accord Lets India Use U.S. Technology," *New York Times*, 18 May 1985.

39. "U.S. Explores Arms Sales to India," *New York Times*, 2 May 1985.

40. "Reagan and Gandhi 'Really Hit It Off,'" *New York Times*, 13 June 1985.

41. Public Relations Officer, Near East–South Asian Affairs, U.S. Department of State, telephone interview with author.

42. Cited in "CM's Evasive Replies Irk Newsmen," *The Hitavada*, 8 December 1984.

Chief Minister Singh could find no reason to fault foreign capital as a whole after the disaster. "I don't think there is any prejudice that has come out of this situation against foreign industry as such – and there should not be" (Arjun Singh, interview with author, 3 March 1985, Bhopal).

43. "Low Farce," *E&PW*, 15 December 1984, p. 1. Amount of bail and plane details from " 'It Was Like Breathing Fire...,' " *Newsweek*, 17 December 1984, p. 12.

E&PW notes, "And lest the U.S. government raise a diplomatic shindy, it has been repeatedly clarified that Prime Minister Rajiv Gandhi had had nothing to do with the decision to 'arrest' the Union Carbide chairman." In an editorial titled "The Shame in Bhopal," the *Sunday Observer* of Bombay (9 December 1984) notes, "The specious plea that Anderson was taken into custody for his own protection does not wash – the state government had ample time to warn the Union Carbide chairman en route in Bombay not to visit Bhopal. The farce of Mr. Anderson's arrest suggests that Mr. Arjun Singh, with or without consulting the prime minister, tried to make political capital out of the visit by Union Carbide officials to Bhopal until the Union government was rudely reminded of the political and economic consequences of arresting an American multinational chairman by the U.S. embassy in New Delhi."

Warren Anderson was charged with culpable homicide not amounting to murder. In addition UCIL officials, including the company's chairman and managing director, and the Bhopal plant works manager and assistant works manager, were arrested under criminal conspiracy, culpable homicide not amounting to murder, causing death by negligence, mischief, mischief in killing of livestock, making atmosphere noxious to health, and negligent conduct in respect to poisonous substances. They were all released on bail. The major offenses carry maximum sentences of life imprisonment. ("Gassed," *The Week*, 16–22 December 1984, p. 18.)

44. Zahreeli Gas Kand Sangharsh Morcha, "Press Statement, 20 December 1984," in Pinto and O'Leary, *Reprints on Union Carbide Chemical Incident*, pp. 16–18.

45. EKLAVYA, "The State of the Environment: A Preliminary Report on the 100th Day After the Gas Disaster" (Bhopal: EKLAVYA, 12 March 1985), p. 1.

46. Ashok Verma, interview with author, 14 February 1985, Bhopal.

47. "Painful Indecision," *India Today*, 31 January 1985.

48. Talmiz Ahmad, interview with author.

49. Cited in "A Matter of 'Faith,' " *The Week*, 30 December–5 January 1985, p. 9.

50. Cited in "No Cause for Panic, CM Allays Fears," *The Hitavada*, 12 December 1984.

51. "Bhopal: Food and Neglect," *The Sunday Observer* (Bombay),